Old Songs Replayed

for Atticus Carr

ISBN: 979-8-218-52446-3

Though Peter Weltner grew up in suburban New Jersey and piedmont North Carolina, his true cultural home was mid-century Manhattan. After graduating from Hamilton College (A.B.) and Indiana University (Ph.D.), he taught in the English Department of San Francisco State for nearly four decades. He has published essays, short stories, novels, and chapbooks and books of poetry. *Old Songs Replayed* is his self-declared fifth "last book." This time he probably means it. He lives in San Francisco near the Pacific with his husband, Atticus Carr.

The two photos of Hamilton College on page 123 are by Richard Lynde, shot in 1961. "The second one, from Dunham Dormitory, was taken," Richard writes, "from my second floor room over the first floor lounge. The snow was associated with a monster Northeaster on January 20/21 and the temperatures ranged from slightly below 0° to the mid-teens in Clinton. A memorable storm."

cover image: "The Yellow Dream" oil on paper, 2000, Galen Garwood

Old Songs Replayed

PETER WELTNER
Poems

marrowstone press

Table of Contents

Letter: Gaius Cilnius Maecenas to Titus Livius (13 B.C.)

"Some years ago my friend Horace described to me the way he made a poem. We had some wine and were talking seriously, and I believe that his description then was a more accurate one than that contained more recently in the so-called Letter to the Pisos—a poem upon the art of poetry of which, I must confess, I am not particularly fond. He said: "I decide to make a poem when I am compelled by some strong feeling to do so—but I wait until the feeling hardens into a resolve, then I conceive an end, as simple as I can make it, toward which that feeling might make progress, though often I cannot see how it will do so. And then I compose my poem, using whatever means are at my command. I borrow from others if I have to—no matter. I invent if I have to—no matter. I use the language that I know, and I work within its limits. But the point is this: the end that I discover at last is not the end I conceived at first. For every solution entails new choices, and every choice poses new problems to which solutions must be found, and so on and on. Deep in his heart, the poet is always surprised at where his poem has gone."

John Williams, *Augustus*

I
Late Winter Snow on College Hill

for the Hamilton College Class of 1964
and
to the Memory of Sam Crowl, '62

Où sont les neiges d'antan?
Where are the snows of years long past?

François Villon, Ballade des dames du temps jadis, from Le Testament

The Campus

Hamilton College. Early sixties. Collegiate
Gothic dorms, classrooms, fraternities
built from local dolomite, a few
of brick smoke-blackened by long,
hard winters. Some New England
scrubbed-clean clapboard houses
with carved wood columns in each corner
of their imposing white wooden porches.
A Victorian mock mini-castle with spired
mimic turret, romantic as a Walter Scott
novel. A cottage, its oldest building,
preserved as an historical relic
for secret meetings by select societies.

Wide swards of grass scrupulously cared for
in warm weather, fields for soccer, lacrosse
a golf course, quads' rolled lawns,
a football field with bleachers seating
two hundred in a small-town-sized stadium
belonging to a campus so expressive
and artful it might be interpretable like a poem,
nearby glens, meadows, woods contributing to its lyricism.

A hill's steep descent to village taverns, a village
green, an inn, the climb back up tough and sobering.

A three story chapel, lead paned windows,
clock and chimes in its steeple, marking
classes and lives, tolling each day's passage
as time moves at its own orderly,
measured, ageless pace in a place like this,
set aside, as if in parentheses,
from the hectic, chaotic, unreflective world
outside it by faith in the grace of knowledge.

1

Curricula

1. Subjects

Homer, Sophocles, Genesis, Shakespeare, Milton,
Racine, Wordsworth, Goethe, Conrad. English.
Greek. Latin. German. French. Spanish.
Philosophy. The core sciences. Mathematics.
Economics. Government. Art history. Public
speaking. Histories of worlds west
and east, north and south. Choral singing.
On stage: Shakespeare, Ben Jonson, Beckett,
Behan. KinoKunst Gesellschaft's movies, silent, classic,
and new wave. A campus newspaper. Creative writing.

2. Place

Towering trees and dorms and fraternities
and quads and a quiet glen whose dew-wet
emerald moss is dappled with morning light
in spring, brilliant like the light of eternity
said by Plato to be glimpsed by thinking
seriously apart from the rest of the world,
by being devoted to reading, pondering, debating,
an ancient Greek ideal made easier maybe
and surely more necessary by the strictures
of winters in upstate New York where snow
and cold and icy roads take a rôle in fostering
the pursuit in knowledge by encouraging those
who are studying to close their doors against
the weather when the sun appears to hover over
the horizon or tree line so low it feels as if morning
begins its part of the day no sooner than late afternoon.

Three Seasons

Autumns composed by Keats, sensuous,
melancholy, enflamed by a forest
of colors, the sober green majesty
of the Mohawk Valley in early fall fast
turning maroon, scarlet, blood orange,
fiery gold until those burning, bleeding
colors slowly fade into November's ashen
grays or earthy browns mingling with
the mud beneath them where they lie
rotting in piles or scattered by winds
over the soft, spongy duff you walk on,
wondering why the beauty of autumn's
dying world turns even more beautiful
when ignited by twilight to reveal itself
like a god in its naked tragic glory.

Winter arrives a week or two after Thanksgiving,
when a few leaves are still clinging to
their branches until they, too, yield
to December's first big snow storm,
the clouds having turned
the pale watery gray of smoke
from a dampened fire.
In time, the snow piles
rise high as second story
windows, or higher, whiter than white
when, under clear skies,
they're lit by moonlight.
Not quite ready to sleep,
you stare out a window, almost transfixed
by the splendor of the scene before you,
like a monk in a monastery contemplating
the mystery of snow: how even in the darkest midnight,
all there is is radiant with light.

Spring appears belatedly, delayed like a love
letter lost in the mail till suddenly
when it arrives
it opens itself
for you to read,
its words far more touching
and surprising than what
you'd hoped for.
As the sun rises over the greening hills
you might fail to notice,
so accustomed you have grown
to snow,
how the morning's light,
the songbirds,
the burgeoning flowers
are inviting you
to leave your rooms,
maybe cut a class or two,
to walk in May's
meadows and woods,
free to do whatever you choose
to do
so long as you bring no books
with you
and ask it no more questions.

Hard Times

1.

Loss, pain, failure, death in its acutest
reality violating our young lives.
A college can't explain or justify
human suffering or do much
to relieve it. Its mission lies elsewhere.

What remains is the unspeakable: new
wars, uprisings, turmoil abroad,
Kennedy's assassination, at this home
or that, yours or another's,
a mother's death, a best friend's suicide.

2.

Right after Thanksgiving in '62, the trees, the streams,
fields, quads, hills turned white. Hopes, fears, dreams,

can sometimes change with the weather The snow
was already heavy in early December, window-

high or higher in places. The crash was a pile-up during a blizzard
on the New York Thruway, like a rupture, a fissure

opening a gap between worlds and times. No one knew what
to do or say after, everyone wondering at first, Is it true?

The next day, the light was a clear, icy white with a blue-cast
to it. But the following evening, another, though lesser blast

from winter blew through, strong enough to fell the tallest tree
in Root Glen. In the storm's dark, no one could see

it topple, a big elm split apart by wind's force and buried
under a mound of white so deep it completely vanished.

Cam, Kit, dead at twenty. The snow just wouldn't quit falling
the night they were killed. The truck driver who hit

their car couldn't see it in the blizzard. Headlights shining
on a snow bank had blinded him. And then there was nothing,
just the vastness of absence, the dread of its silence.

Root Glen

One cold March night, warmed by heavy coats, scarves, hats,
strong Scotch, friends and I wandered across a bridge
over an icy creek in Root Glen and gazed up at the sky
through a solitary gap in the trees' bleak, winter-bare
branches to see what Coleridge had seen a century
and a half before and written about soon after in a poem
George Nesbitt had read aloud to us early that Friday
morning. We looked up, searched a while until there it was:
"the hornèd moon with one bright star within the nether tip."

Come, friends. Walk with me to the glen again. Let us gaze up
at the sky together all these years later to see how it still shines, that
star, immutably in the nether tip of Coleridge's inspiriting crescent moon.

College Hill Road and Root Hall

On a winter night's piercing cold, I climbed up College Hill
knowing where to go only by following the chapel's light
the snow flurries blurred and diffused like a sheet filtering
candle light in a game of ghosts boys play to frighten each other.

Colin Miller's young son was piping bagpipes
further up the hill, the music seeming
to come from as far away as the highlands,
the plaintive tune he was playing barely
as audible as the snow's sibilant whisperings,
the trees' limbs being battered, twisted by winds.

The few guys I passed leaned against the gusts
like hovering shadows, caps pulled low,
their hands gloved, their faces up to their eyes
wrapped in scarves, blurring where they were going.
Back on campus, I heard and saw no one else
as I tried not to slip or fall on the slick, icy paths.

Halfway across campus, I quit struggling against
the wind and waited until my watery, teary eyes
cleared before I took another step.

Out of the moonless, starless dark,
right before me, shockingly,
Root Hall rose into sight,
as if it had just been born
out of the snow
like Atlantis
out of the sea,
white and red and silvery,
thousands upon thousands
of snowflakes, like froth
churned up by a whirlpool.
spinning, prancing, swirling, twisting,
dancing around it.

Back at the house, exhausted, I almost fell
while struggling to open its door,
weighty and arched like a monastery's.
Inside, I stripped off my outer clothes
to warm myself by a fire in the library
while guys in the Long Room,
a little high from days of being
cooped up and drinking lots
of late night scotches,
were laughing and shouting and partying,
while listening to the Shirelles and Shangri-Las.

Why was I elated by what I had seen
while fighting myself through the snowstorm?
Looking through cupped hands
and frosted, lead-paned windows,
I contemplated the snow as it fell slowly,
heavily, steadily over all the earth,
claiming it, possessing it, as it does at the end
of Joyce's story about the dead,
as if I, too. had had a vision
of something ominously, transcendently beautiful,
in the midst of the cold of a blinding blizzard.

House Parties and Frat Houses

Thirteen hundred years ago, the poet Wei Ying-wu
wrote of boats docked while waiting in a storm
for clearer days, vessels that might never
pass his way again; of a House of Pleasure,
lovely as a silk screen, he used to visit daily
when he was young but, old, goes to no more,
bereft at heart for all he's had to leave behind:
the rice wine the Emperor's soldiers left
unspoiled and undrunk, the friends he'd made,
the swallows that fluttered like blue-green petals
caught in rain, buffeted by winds, flying toward summer.
If I were denied my desires, Wei writes, how could I
know pleasure? Denied my wine, how could I learn sobriety?

The Chapel

And old Wei wrote about how the sun as it sinks
deepens thought. Dreams recur. Memories return,
until a late night wind snatches them away
to carry them heavenward. In winter, the sleet,
frost, snow are white with one grief. Age, he complains,
has exiled him. He aches. The shrine is tangled
with ivy. When he hikes through woods, its shadows
pursue him. Do birds at twilight feel freed from time?
All the monks, scholars he once knew are strangers now,
but even so he listens keenly while the monastery chimes out
its ritual hours to the somber sound of its big bronze bells.
He waits by the temple's gate where glittering hungry fish feed.
If paradise grew old too, would it be as passionate as he feels now?
Will the day come when he'll bury his sorrows to the sound of tolling bells?

After the Last Exams

Earth was paradise enough, a happiness present in everyday
pleasures. May elated us. Why study more? The warmth that
had melted the ice and snow in late April had missed spots
among the shadows in Rogers Woods or Root Glen. But
at dawn, after a night's soft rain, the forest glowed. Our bikes
sped down paths through the college by brookside willows,
sycamore, maples, oaks, and birches as we rode side by
side, never racing, being careful of traces of late winter
dangers lingering in muddy patches not yet dried by the sun.
The leaves were pastel green. Bee balm, cardinal flower,
red trillium. He could identify them all. Clouds in a blue sky
billowed with showers to come, the linen-white lilac, dewy
trillium, crocus all in bud. We lolled on the quad's rolled lawn until
the sun reddened into a twilight in that final springtime, knowing
he'd soon go his way, I mine, into our separate lives of silent remembering.

Graduation

1.

It is about two o'clock the last night I will sleep
on campus. Later that day is graduation.
A fire smoldering in the hearth is warming
the bed where I rest in the chill of a windy
room in a house built of thick beams and heavy stone.
I hear music outside and a voice singing. I open
a window to see better. It's a calm, clear night,
yet, though it's late May, the light the moon
sheds looks like snow falling in January, like lunar snow,
elusive and fragile as it looms over and drifts onto
the flowers blossoming below my window, welcoming
the moon at night as they would the sun by day,
unfurling every petal to its cool, gentle, melting light.

2.

Do you remember Ed Barrett's telling his class
that Shakespeare's Puck with his tricks
and wand was able to make all right,
to fix all his mistake by play's end,
because it revealed, as Prospero's rough
magic would later, imagination's power
to awaken slumbering lives into reality?
As we left his class on a mid-winter noon
a year before we'd finished our studies,
the sun, breaking fast through clouds,
was reflected by the snow shining so
brightly into the classroom it hurt our eyes,
briefly blinding us, like theater lights
turned on suddenly after the show's over.
We blinked and rubbed our eyes,
trying to see a way out, to find the door
while Ed laughed and spread his arms
out wide as he could reach, as if meaning
to sprinkle us all with juice he'd squeezed

from Puck's love-in-idleness so that we'd be
translated too, like the midsummer lovers
near the end of the play, never to need to leave
this place nor ever weep, transfixed by the magic of Shakespeare's art.

Two Photos Taken in Winter, 1963

1.

The picture is aged and faded, with a golden
glow to it like an aura of epilogue.
I hold it closer to my eyes. Two streaks
of bright red and ultramarine, like stripes
on flags or waving long pennants, flow
from each upper corner onto a scene
in the midst of a December storm. The light
is hazy, as if it's being filtered through gauze.
(Imagine the earth beneath the snow exhaling
its hot breath into the chilly air above it.)
Head-high, boulder-wide snowbanks lie piled
beside roads and walkways. There's no one
in the photo. The hushed, breath-like rush of falling
snow is stilled into a world too snow-bound to see.

2.

The sky is a sleek cloudless blue, clear as over
a sea. The storm's blown through. A moon,
thin and pale yellow, lingers above a stand
of oak. It is a peaceful morning, like music
played faraway. Glinting like crystal from
last night's ice, the trees serve as sentinels
for the cemetery, casting shadows on
the rime- and snow-covered tombstones
as if they're mourning the souls that rest
below them. There is no other expression
of sorrow in the photo nor of regret. Yet,
as I stare at it, my eyes seem to search for
something below the snow, a tie, a wool scarf,
a ring, a pin, any clue to what I've lost, any memento.

Herkimer Dolomite

1.

Hunched, arthritic, his clothes reeking from
cigar smoke, an old man visits the Sig house
bearing tweeds, an itinerant tailor who sews
suits, jackets, slacks for young gentlemen,
his fabrics woven only from highland wools,
he says, their colors a subtle thistle, loch blue.
But times have changed. He finds no buyers, shrugs,
and stacks his goods in the back of his coupe,
drives down College Hill Road, his cloth bolts
piled up like rolled up banners behind his seat.

2.

It's twilight in late February, the sky's bronze,
as if rusted with age, the luminous coppery
brown of decaying leaves or the campus'
dolomite buildings that sparkle at dusk.
The pits where their stones were dug from
are quarried out. What rock is left to mine
lacks iron, won't rust, stays dull gray despite
years of weathering, not worth cutting
into blocks to fix what is chipped or cracked
on the college's gothic edifices, stained by
a century and a half of northern New York ice storms.

3.

I first saw them in spring, young men playing lacrosse
in the quad by the chapel, the morning light
casting over dorms a ruddy patina, sun
soaked, like the mid-May tan on the guys
pitching, catching the ball with their racquets.
It's odd how vividly I recall them that one time,
three months before I enrolled, like a picture visited
often before in a scrapbook seen more vividly years later.

4.

In October's loveliest days, the Mohawk Valley's
dense, dark woods turn a velvety scarlet,
fiery red, burnished gold, bold flickering
yellows like a shrine's votive candles or hearth
flames slowly dying to November's embers, ash
pale or flakey white, omens of what's ahead.
In upstate, winters are long and hard, the sky
the watery, inky gray from the storm-heavy,
fierce clouds that possess it. But the old
cut blocks of dolomite thrive in cold, their colors
intensifying, blushed by the rust hidden in stone,
not diminished by time, but enhanced by it to a kind
of glory, as if the overcoming of loss and death might
be chiseled and hewn from stone to reveal a smoldering beauty.

5.

Michelangelo carved to free bodies lost, hidden, in marble.
He understood why stone memories last far longer than
men's. No matter the season, the campus' dolomite buildings
glitter like crystalline snow, like the ancient eyes of the old
men Yeats saw looking upon a tragic scene with a cold
detachment that concealed the inner burning that fired their sight.
Those college buildings' sparkling façades conceal deep veins.
What if life also rusted like iron to a color the golden
bronze of the stones of the old, stoic buildings we lived
in and among for years, our lasting home, our mineral companions?

In Memoriam

after Horace: Odes, Book 4, 7: Diffugere nives

Snow is fast fleeing before earth's greening
as trees unfold their leaves to breathe
new air. The tremulous earth is changing
once more as rivers, flowing seaward, seethe
and churn and race each other home. The Graces
and lovely, nymph-like girls dance naked,
but last past June no longer than songbirds, bees,
or golden children playing in meadows. It's said,
beyond the Styx, a man's just mist. The seasons
show us why. The earth is ever repeating.
The sun melts winter, burns away spring.
Autumn offers its harvest, its apples and damsons
and pears, then vanishes into winter's tenacious cold
and sunlessness, though each returns again,
like the moon to the sky. But not us. Young or old,
we die. Not ours to come and go like snow or rain.
Heroic, pious Aeneas, rich, royal Tullus, Ancus,
King of Rome, turn to dust and shadows.
Who knows what careless Time unfolds for us?
The gods will give what they have given. No one follows
them skyward. Vibrant, joyous soul, now you've died
and Minos has judged you as the rare, good man
you were, you'll still not come back. No one's been revived
from death's stony clutches, its icy grip since life began.
Not even Diana can save her beloved chaste Hippolytus,
restore him to the light. Nor can brave, storied Theseus
break the chain of forgetfulness that encloses Pirithous
in its iron prison, his dear friend lost to him, like you to me, Torquatus.

Convocation, September, 1960

"Where, oh, where are the pea green freshmen…?"

Sitting in the three story chapel, austere, protestant,
thin maroon velvet cushions on dark, hard pews,
white walls and columns, framed clear panes, sent
there by hope, I suppose, listening to news
of our lives now, two hundred boys and more
learning the traditions, rules we'll have obeyed
or not before we leave while from outside, a door
of the chapel, half open, the aureate light, unfaded,
of early fall pours in, the chill air, summer over,
we breathe in, not knowing what will become
of us, strolling to our rooms in Dunham, the thrill
of debating the future, our lives ahead, not yet summoned
by the first hints of autumn on the Hill to be brought
to bloom some day like trees with snow in nearby woods each winter.

Gaudeamus igitur

Let us be joyful when we
are young, and happy.
Old age will deny
us youth's pleasures.

Where have they gone,
our old companions?
Their lives are done.
Ours go on.

Life is brief, soon over,
no one spared
death's power.
But why despair?

Drink wine, Drink beer.
Make love, Let
fear disappear
in high spirits.

Long live our college. Long live
its teachers, what they give
us students
and our descendants.

May all who love and cherish
learning sing a hymn
to knowledge,
that it never perish.

Praise charity, its many
benefactors. May there be
no sorrow
or anguish tomorrow.

May evil die and violence and haters,
the world be filled
with lovers.
Let no more blood be spilled.

And so, to close, let's praise
our campus
for all it taught us. Raise
your glasses high, singing Gaudeamus.

Late Winter Snow on College Hill

Bits and pieces. A jumble. A gallimaufry.
Images. Faces. Bodies. Names.
Buildings. Our past together summoned
by pictures of us young as I flip through

pages of yearbooks, seeking
memories to link us, like an arc
to bridge eras, like a note, a letter,
a few words that might matter. Or photos.

I'm insecure about the truth of all
I've recalled, about how fallible I am,
how forgetful at times
as memories begin to vanish

like surviving snow in trees' shadows until
it slowly thaws in spring while pale
green leaves are fast unfurling
and flowers blossoming in glens and meadows.

Where are the snows of yesteryear? Snow can be
beautiful, snow can be tragic like memories,
like the swallows resting in a snowy field we saw long
ago staring back at us through the cold transparency of winter air.

Twilight in Winter

In his faraway world, the poet Du Mu wrote,
autumn is nearly over, lofty clouds mingling
with the sun's weak rays. Then cold skies
arrive, weighty with frost and snow. He must

move on, go elsewhere, never to return here.
He hears the field below where he stands wailing
with the ghosts of lost companions. Heavy
clouds press down on him as daylight falters.

A swift snow dances in the swirling wind. There's
no good wine left in the cask in his house, though
his hearth fires flicker red as he composes
poems to be spoken to the empty air. From friends

he hears not a word, yet there's a chill white lucency,
like jade's, to the moon tonight, like bells mourning
in a temple or migrating birds in their final flight
from winter until dusk submits to a darkened earth.

If he were to go this night, he'd leave no footprints
in the snow, so light and ghost-like he feels,
like a distant memory returning to him as he wakes from
dreaming of a sun rising toward paradise on a cold, clear morning.

An Open Book

1. Mohawk Valley

The best way to see it is to hike the hill
up to a clearing overlooking the Mohawk
Valley, the sky icy blue in the chill
morning air, a few cirrus clouds chalk
white and floating slowly out of sight.
The leaves glow crimson, rust, golden,
fleshy orange, lemon rind in a last rite
of October, tapestries elaborately woven,
yet with no discernible pattern, free,
spontaneous, the light they emanate bright
as a kaleidoscope's without its geometry.
In a remote grove of spruce and hickory,
a rivulet from yesterday's rains trickles
through weeds, over roots, rocks, and twigs.

A fat gray squirrel ponders nuts the hickories
have dropped near it and with its paws digs
in the earth, gnaws one, climbs an oak. Half-
hidden in a thicket, a red fox sniffs, suspecting
human presence, frozen as a photograph
until it scampers through leaves and brush rustling
at its flight. Spruce and hickory, gray
squirrel, red fox, a rivulet skirting a boulder:
all must, as soon as tomorrow or the day
after, like fall's leaves' embers that still smolder
below first snows, succumb to winter. What will stay
permanent? In old age, the mind is stripped bare
like woods in autumn preparing for the coming winter.
Do not grieve. The world you leave behind will greet you there.

2. Rogers Woods

And so spring comes again, as after every winter
it must, trees unfolding new leaves under skies
the soft white blue of antique porcelain,
the air shimmering to the sound of the chapel's

bells, flowers budding here and there, wild
or gardened, dew glistening on grass
freshly greening, winged seeds lifted by
morning's breezes; and you, book in hand,

going to a class as if your studies will be
enhanced by how spring's re-emergent
passions renew thought, too, take their part
in learning and its pursuit of reason, fact,

and clarity. Later, loafing in Rogers Woods,
you lie on a patch of dry ground and soft
grass near a small pool of late thawed snow
and stare up through a gap in the trees' canopy

hoping to find in the darkening sky some sign
of what you'd studied that day in a class
on Keats' odes, wondering if any twilight
could ever truly rhyme with the poet's

sorrowing, romantic summoning of a temple
of delight where veil'd Melancholy has her
sovran shrine, when suddenly a flock of
white-spotted blackbirds flies over your head

as if they were the birds in flight brushed in ink
on a Chinese screen you'd been shown that
afternoon in an art history class, now freed from
an ancient silk screen's imagery to soar over the college.

II.

Renderings

To render: to melt down, to extract by melting, to treat so as to convert into other material, to transmit, to deliver, to give up, yield, to hand down a judgement, to agree on a verdict, to give back, restore, to reflect, echo. to give in acknowledgment, to pay, to do a service, to make, to depict, to produce a copy or version of, to administer, to apply plaster or cement to, to translate.

From Latin re-dare, to give back, to Old French rendre, to Middle English render.

The earliest senses were 'recite', 'translate', and 'give back' (hence 'represent' and 'perform'); 'hand over' (hence 'give help' and 'submit for consideration'); 'cause to be'; and 'melt down.'

Thera

1.

On grotto walls, in frescos they've survived.
Boys boxing, hooked fish, a silver unicorn,
blue birds, monkeys, cinch-waisted, bare-breasted
women. Listen. Krimon calls to Amotion

who's racing to him. In a cave, after making
love, they cut their names like graffiti
in the rock face of a mountain, left nothing
but ruins when it blew into the sea.

2.

Sunrise. He longs for Apollo, his light
to come, for love, its daybreak brilliance
to enter him. Cloudless skies, the insight
that comes from perfect days, the radiance

of the sea-, whitewashed Cyclades. His holiday
is almost over, his summer's devotion.
Thera's taught him to worship, to pray
to the Mediterranean as if to Poseidon.

Women's hoop earrings, braided hair,
skirts embroidered like tapestries,
their graceful dancing, wine, bright fair
skin, almond eyes. Floral intricacies,

lithe ferns, dolphins flying over ships
oared to harbor. Sienna dark men,
handsome, bold shoulders, string-thin lips,
blue hair, black ringlets. He lived well then.

Its grapes still sweeten his tongue. The sun
is white, the sea tarnished copper's blue-greens,
still water's silver mirror. The island's a profusion
of tesserae, fragments of ancient scenes,

the man he'd been four millennia before
his birth, found, restored, images
exposed or extracted from rubble like ore
from a pit, carved names, chiseled messages.

3.

By Delphinios, Krimon had sex with a boy,
the brother of Bathykles. Timagoras and O.
and Empheres had sex here. Older than Troy,
scratched into Mesa Vouno, the names
of men like him in the throes of their first joy.

Kallisté. Most beautiful island. Sacred
to Zeus, the Charities, Persephone, Hermes,
a crescent moon seaborne, naked
as these lovers (say their names
as ours): Rheksanor, Arkhagetas, Prokles.

Uruk

1.

The Milky Way consists of a hundred billion stars or more,
the number mind-numbing, the distance unthinkable.
Where I stand alone, close to shore, massive waves
swell and crash with little resistance from the cliffs.
A big storm is due to hit just hours from now, threatening
to batter the coast with gale-force winds, toppling trees,
flattening dunes. The moon glowers down on the surging
sea, the sky star-lit and unclouded. It is unfathomable
how ever-recurring-night rolls on and on and yet changes
as people must move in the land of the dead, forever the same,
yet restless and hovering, their lives never done with. I stare
up at the sky, searching for more signs of the storm on its way.
As I wait, I picture a constellation, now no more seen by us
in the heavens, the people who named it long gone, too.
I imagine its form, what myths it might have been given, what
truths it was once thought to convey, whatever its light might mean.

2.

So Gilgamesh wanders the earth always, ever in search
of what he yearns for. Something huge is missing,
not just love, now that Enkidu's dead. But to reach
deep into the sea and to find what he needs, diving

into the ensuing flood of life, deep deep to the bottom,
to discover the plant, promised, that could be
his salvation, not his lover—no, not him,
not anymore—but the flower of heartbeat, immortality

riddled with thorns and nettles that the sea monster,
the monstrous sea, all of it, snatches away
from his grip before he can taste it, high water
and winds whirling him in the storm, and he their prey

31

until back in Uruk, in lives ages later, as the last day's sun
slips behind his palace's gates, he sees rising
the sign that Ptolemy will later name Orion,
in his tongue, Uru An-Na, hunter,
                    bull-fighter,
                        the light of heaven,
    undying.

A Kore Found on Paros by Linda

Imagine a day you cherish is a child on her way to some kingdom,
unaware, smiling as she might after being given a treat
by her mother for no reason, a pretty comb,
a frilly bow, a kiss, a compliment. The spring's heat
turns droplets of sweat into beads on her arms and forehead.
She's wearing a flowery, floppy bonnet to protect
her from the mid-day sun whose glare, she's read
somewhere, might burn her exposed skin and infect
her mind with desires, longings, she, out of innocence,
must never know of. Say that wondrous day, its memory in the present,
is also in danger, like the girl who lives near by you whom no one would sense
to be at risk from idly roaming, playing in a meadow until, while bent
over to pick a peony hidden by ivy and weeds, she is raped, abducted,
into night and death by a ravenous old man, thrust into the ignominy
of her shame and his oblivion, forgotten by all but her mother, the ancient story she
tells you of why only grieving could save her child, like your lost days, from silence.

Homer

to the memory of Bill Chaplin

Your imagination's drawn to rosy Greek dawns, to the Greek
sea: grape pulp dark, dark as dregs in a wine
cup. Ram-headed, dolphin-eyed, swordfish sleek,
a ship—bow, hull, sails—is painted a golden incarnadine
by the rising sun—like statues, columns in a shrine
to Apollo whose eyes burn into morning, seeing what he
alone can see. A reed boat floats by the coastline
where you stand, back to Troy, delighting in the mist,
the hints of a breeze, the slight chill of the sea-
surge on your body, reluctant to wade in it while wisps
of night linger, dripping in caves, and the cries of gulls
pierce through you like the ululations of warriors mourning
their fallen; like the ancient, scraggy voice of a man who pulls
you back toward the underworld you dread, who begs, Pour me more
blood to drink and I'll tell you their story. By beached ships, you are waiting
to hear it once more, its dawn-song, its first-light splendor, its sea-borne terror.

Homage to Catullus

1.

Remember Sirmio, Gellius, that jewel of peninsulas
and islands jutting into the sapphire blue
of Benacus, where you took me, the days
we spent there because you'd read Catullus?
What drew you to me, a poor poet? Days
of bliss, all cares set aside as if two strangers
had found a new home in a longed-for bed,
no secrecy, no need to hide. How many nights,
how many times did we come inside each other,
neither slave nor master? The comfort, joy, end
to labor, the easy laughter of our days spent
in ancient ways made us pagans, I suppose,
in the poet's Sirmio, reveling in the Lydian waves
of sacred Garda. By what right can one claim
another's words for his own? As we fucked each
other, was each of us telling a lie? Nothing
can be the same between one time and another.
Search, explore, reach for it as you like, the past
is untranslatable, like any summer you might name
you yearn to return to, like you to me, like us to Sirmio,
because, millennia later, you dreamed you might be
remembered as the man who could write erotic poetry,
not knowing whether you'd been meant to ascribe to yourself
the part of betrayer or betrayed, beloved or bitter, thwarted lover.

2.

Though attempting to render
Callimachus's verses for you,
Gellius, remember
that no matter how true,
faithful I want to be, how diligently
I've set to work, someone
is always shooting arrows
at them and not them alone,
but at me, too. I fear
my labors are all in vain,
that my pleas were useless here.
It's like two lovers, you and me
for instance.   We hail aspersions, let rain
down curses, as if there were no penalty
to pay for our folly,
the joyous cruelty we heap on one another.

Virgil, after Aeneid, Book VI

The descent famously irreversible, the bough
the tree gives him, the way down the earth
shows him, the passages in Homer it reminds
him of, the images it evokes, the grove that lights
his way as if leaves could shine like torches by
the cave's mouth, the haunting sound of long
missed voices whispering, murmuring, the spirit
that glows from ghosts like twilight in woods,
their tears, what grieves underground in an echoing
grotto like a world recalled he knows, Troy,
the past he's lost, its forests burned or chopped,
toppled, his last glimpse of it, its towers on
fire (think courthouse, school, steeple wherever
you live, all ablaze), his journeys over the sea,
the plains where he fought to stay, and now this,
these shades he hears sighing to him as if from
wind-carved craters or a deep abyss saying,
Every man's fate is a disaster for even you who
are alive must move restlessly as water, flicker
like us in subterranean caverns, never to be free,
our names eroded by rain and wind from every
tomb or monument, erased from every page,
you, hero, who cannot know in the days to follow
what might befall you save for missing the friends
and companions Death has taken from you, a city
to found, a new Ilium, wanting to return home
history reversed, that dream impossible to realize
since all you believed had worth in your stored,
fallen city is irredeemable by an imperial Rome
that will never know peace despite its power and majesty.
Once you've left us, Aeneas, forget us and never look back.

Virgil, after Georgics, 2

The famished animals, creatures of field and forest—
buffalo, deer, sheep, heifer—eagerly devour
the boy-god's vines and ivy, but are far less
ravenous than the beasts whose venomous teeth
greedily rip and tear, gnaw and gnash at stems
and leaves, feeding on greenery in an oppressive heat.

Theirs are the blasphemies for which Bacchus requires
the sacrifice of a young, virile goat.
                                  Ancient theater
began in these earliest rites, in song contests
and satyric dances whose members were disguised
in oiled goatskins, each enactor wearing a mask
carved from green wood, chanting randily mocking verses

as they sang to a fearless Bacchus, wild child, frenzied,
perpetually ageless adolescent, master-mistress
of transmutations, recalling his lyrics of spring,
hanging propitious false phalluses on branches
of oak trees, swaying with them as they swung in breezes
while the god's snake-like vines ripened and entwined them, flourishing.

So bring forth your fruit, child god. Let every meadow, field,
darkened woods, sprawling farmland, every stream and river
break free to liberate our lives, while we, since it is right and meet
to do so, sing and grasp the chosen one, the goat-god, by his painted horns
and lead him to the place set aside for sacrifice where we roast his flesh
and eat his meat on spits of smoky hazel wood, crackling cypress,
sappy resinous pine.

Horace, Odes 3, 13: O fons Bandusiae

Font, wellspring of sacrifice, Bandusian fountain
to which is brought seasonal libations of wine, offerings
of flowers that the fields be rich with grain,
that rain fall abundantly, that nothing be done in vain
when the chosen first born of the flock, its horns foretelling
the future, is slaughtered, staining your splendid waters, coloring
them red while the cruel heat of Canicula, dog-star, pounds
on their farms, yet cannot pierce through the glade
where the people are gathered, cannot penetrate the shade
that saves them from prostration and ruin because of the inviting
coolness of its canopy,

oh, fons Bandusiae, clearer than crystal, see
for yourself, listen: the sounds
of the procession grow louder as it approaches, the plodding
cattle, the weary oxen, the wandering,
late-pasturing flock with the lamb, the lamb, the chosen lamb
violently struggling, protesting against its yoke and harness,
strong for one so young, percipient as an old ram
who's survived many such ceremonies; aquarian vessel, it is I who bear witness
to your fame among fountains, though I would here praise instead, sing
only of the berried Ilex tree rooted below the low marble wall that surrounds
you, yet whose branches aspire higher that your leaping waters ever could or can.

Horace, Odes 1, 8: Lydia, dic per omnis

For heaven's sake, Lydia, you love the wrong man and you
love him wrongly. Sybaris used to adore, even worship
the playing field, any parade ground or new
challenge at manly games, always eager to strip
off his fancy civvies and don heavy arms. A riotous
sun pounding down on his naked, sweaty body never
troubled him. Fighting in weather's worst was a plus.
Remember how he swam against the rushing Tiber
and won? His aplomb with bit and bridle lightly riding
his horse? Now he is nearly terrified of anointing
himself with oil as if it were the poison of a snake.
He's run away. I can't find him. Why do his muscles
show no fresh bruises or wounds? What have you done? Wake
up, Lydia I hear he's hiding seaside dressed like Achilles
in women's clothes as if they might keep him from the war
which, after all, despite your tears, was what you'd loved him for.

Horace, Odes, 1, 31: Quid dedicatum poscit Apollinem

Let him pray to divine Apollo in his luminous temple.
Let him pour new wine from a crystal bowl
in ritual sacrifice, not to petition for the people
of Sardinia to be blessed with a rich harvest, fertile
as its soil is, nor to ask for gold or ivory—the toll
wealth takes far too cruel when one possesses it—
nor for their grazing, content herds be turned to fatted cattle
to sell. Let him not seek for the meadows and fields that sit
peacefully beside a rippling, placidly flowing Liris river
to be anything more than a place to rest and take in the view
as it flows down and through the Apennines he once loved and knew
so well, like the Calenian grapes he pruned with little hooks when much younger.

No, let him pray instead that the earth be well, that good order
and fortune bless all of those who prune their vines
carefully anywhere, who grow grapes that lack
any bitterness because they nurture them artfully, wines
more inspiring than any some rich merchant just back
from Syria would pour into the gold cup he holds in his hands
too proudly, knowing nothing of what it means to taste and savor its delights.

And let him pray, as fervently, to the god who understands
the dangers faced by all who sail upon the Atlantic,
who risk its waves, who journey on it even further
than brave Ulysses ever dared, a plain man who time
after time came back safely to relish his return to land, climb
hills, swim, enjoy a simple meal of hickory and mallow
and olives picked from a grove near where brightly yellow
lemons emitted their sharp, sweet scent, pungent and acidic.
Let him pray that now, this late, he sleep nights in the same bed, restless no more.

Apollo, law-giver, god of light and wolves and music
and mice, grant that he at the end be at last content,
no more a wanderer. Let him know that if he grow sick
in his old age, you will show him from the firmament
where you dwell why it, the seas, rivers, lakes, meadows,
the roads and highways, the fields, cities, all places of human labor
are worthy of equal praise when seen though your clarifying splendor,
so that he, this old man, having lived, survived to the end of his days
if not with honor, at least as one who was able to do his work in the only ways
he knew how, honoring the sacred, profitless things of rhyme and form and lyric.

Horace, Odes, Book 1, 24: Quis desiderio sit pudor
  for David Morris

What language is given us, where can we learn to mourn
the dead without shaming them or us, to revive those
who will never wake again? Our poet has been borne
into the underworld, its crooked shadows, its dire clothes
of mist and fog. Not even Orpheus playing his lyre,
to whom deaf trees would listen, can restore the life
of a shade. Quintilius sleeps forever while a civic pyre
burns to his memory, unfelt in the cold, dreamless, strifefree
world of death below. No music, even his, can persuade
the gods to open stone doors they've closed forever. Teach
me the art, Melpomene, to bring him back to us, unafraid
of dying twice. Or at least teach me how to mourn, how to reach
Fate's ears so Truth might change its mind. Or must I endure
to live the rest of my days in despondency with a grief that has no cure?

Horace, Odes, 1,10: Mercuri, facunde nepos Atlantis
for Robert Mohr

Winged message-bearer, great-grandson of the sea,
border-maker, border-breaker, thief, deceiver,
beautiful, heroically phallic, it was you, Mercury,
who gave to the wild, savage ones the gift of order

through language and speech and the grace of play,
even the ground rules by which wrestlers wrestled
as if each match owed to you who would win the day
according to your wisdom so that they might have settled

their senseless wars. Lyre-inventor, sweet musician, honey-
tongued lover, charmer, you enjoyed hiding.
Remember when you stole, on a glorious, sunny
day, Apollo's cattle, while they were idly grazing,

right from under his watchful eyes? It made him laugh,
how bold you were, how much you understood
the crush he had on you, its power against his wrath,
though he pretended to storm and rage, as a god should,

against you, threatening to send his arrows' lightning
down upon you. And that time, near war's end,
when you showed Priam—weary and old, bearing
his few unscorched clothes, a pocket of gold—how to wend

his way safely through the Thessalian lines, watchfires,
and guards to the other side of their camp to die, happily,
in peace? It is what you give to all, the god who esquires
the dead like a servant to where they must go to find home, to be

at rest. Maybe it is a place of bliss, who knows? You
wave your golden wand, play your lyre, even sing,
I suppose, until the gods above and below know how much it's true:
obscurity is who you are and mystery and the love whose every night is morning.

Horace, Odes 1, 3: Sic te diva potens Cypri

May Venus, of Cythera, of Cyprus, who knows
how many other Grecian islands, the Dioscuri,
twins shining in untroubled heavens, bestow
on you safe journey, Virgil, the sky
as clear as it is here today. What man
first dared to risk the seas, the wrath
and vagaries of Poseidon's winds? Land
is the birthright of humanity; the path
of life's journey is surest, clearest when
earthbound. Monsters swim in the sea.
Cliffs crumble into it. It dooms men
to a dreadful end. It was an impiety
to transgress the waters that divide
us. Yet heroes repeatedly seek the forbidden,
what's denied them. Questing Prometheus, allied
with no one, acquiring fire. Daedalus, wearing
wings of his devising, aspiring to fly
too high. Laboring Hercules, descending
into death's kingdom, risking imprisonment. Why
risk it, Virgil? Why write as you do, so beautifully
and surely as if daring the gods to abuse
you of your powers, hurling cruel lightning,
thunderbolts against you and your journeys
with Aeneas. Take care on your way
to Greece, my friend, to that audacious, original place
of our art. The Greeks knew more than we about
the anger of gods, the dark destinies you retrace
in your poem, so that even those who are devout
in their observance of the rites, as we are to our poetry,
shall come to see how much life's greatness owes to its tragedy.

To Quintus Horatius Flaccus

Death is indifferent in its ferocious immensity. It stupefies
the mind with its cruelties, defying all words. Each day,
I take a walk along the shore. By dawn, I watched
a crow pecking at the carcass of a gull, bloodying
the wet sand at low tide's edge. Fish heads, crab shells,
a few beached bottles lay scattered in the dune grass.
I remembered a story Linda had told me decades ago.
How she had found on a mountain in Paros a shard
of a kouros she had fallen in love with at first sight.
How she kissed his lips, sun-warmed and inviting to hers.
How her blood quickened with pleasure. Why she feared nothing.
Two homeless men doze snoring on a bench. A frisky dog
barks at the rumbling roar of waves breaking near where it plays.
We savor the wine we're given, Horace wrote, despite our live's inconsequence.

The Fates and Fame of Two Augustan Poets

I Publius Ovidius Naso

1.

I recall, confused, beasts being slaughtered to feast
Augustus' fawning cronies, slaves carrying roast boars
on their shoulders to the tables where his guests
lounged, gossiping, Spanish courtesans standing
half-hidden in veiled corners, scented with rose
water, hibiscus, grape leaves, slaves dancing
nearly naked, women, boys driven to frenzy by timbrels,
flutes, drums, crotales. All this excess, Caesar savored
and despised just as he confusingly exiled poets for
their writings' licentiousness while otherwise admiring them
or doomed his beloved daughter to endure an island's solitude
for lustily flinging herself at dozens of men. The emperor is
a man of wanton contradictions, the peace he seeks that leads to
the deaths of thousands thousands of solders in Dacia, Parthia, North Africa.

2.

And so I will die by his command, too, alone, along a craggy
shoreline where a fisherman is tying up a small boat
dockside as I watch it rock in the sea's gentle waves
like a cradle. My days pass in boredom. How freely
I used to pour wine at parties, yet also solemnly,
like a rite to a god who's owed his own ceremonies
for the pleasures he's given you. Beyond the Black Sea's
shores lie the lands of unlatined, untutored barbarians
whom I fear for their hated of Rome while plots are still
being concocted against me at home, though I am a man
of no importance now, a once celebrated poet known
for how I saw everything in life, as in death, metamorphosing,
transforming in ways comic and tragic: as exile has changed
me into a ghost shuffling among lemures and the restless living dead.

3.

Many ancient Greeks, I'm told, believed that language
began in songs of mourning, in ululations. Do any Romans
think that today? Might my poetry be read in future
ages long after the man who wrote them has been
forgotten by history? This morning, I found a shard of Greek
pottery and saved it for good luck. When I
die, who will pour wine on my grave, offer me,
as an oblation, lemon cakes and honeyed almonds?
I sense the willful chill of Olympian silence passing
through me. The only home I know now is this
solitary, barren state of old age, the years I've wasted
in exile. I subside on melons, dates, figs, choke on local
wines. Wave after wave laps at my feet as I wait like a fool
for sight of the ship that, before it's too late, will take me back to Rome.

II *Drusus Marius Falco*

1.

In the Caucasus, a woman, her black hair sun gritty,
and her cracked-faced craggy farmer husband
are bound to the land's life more than their own.
Each day they climb steep, zigzagging paths
back to their bed, the old woman dressed head
to toe in black, her aging husband limping, halt,
stumbling as he follows her to the summit
where they dwell like their ancestors whose names
they recite as if they were mantras or prayers
to protect them in this life and guide them to a better
one after they've died. The couple works their spare,
tiered fields for enough grain to sustain life. They irrigate
the infertile soil with rain water gathered in cisterns. Their hut
sits under trees by a sacred cave it's forbidden for the living to enter.

2.

No complete lines by Marius have survived, just fragments
faded, rotted, on a page of a papyrus scroll in a tin
cylinder discovered on a hunch by a scholar hidden
in a dry cave behind a peasants' hut on a steep hill
near the Black Sea, a scroll that became notorious
for a poem in superior condition that its discoverer
thought at first to have been composed by Ovid,
its style so like his, during his exile in Tomis. The scroll's
shorter poem, attributed in it to an otherwise
mysterious Drusus Marius Falco, was considered by
latinists too fragmentary to matter. Nothing is known
about Marius. Merely a few hundred blurred words have
survived him, like these that had the good sense to be
entombed for two millennia with lines fine enough to be Ovid's.

3.

Our cohort   centurion   leave Rome   tomorrow
to fight   Dacian.   Parthian borders   Caesar
who can know   passion   fiercer than a sunset
over sea   Catullus wrote to Juventius
that lovers   to be true must betray one
another   set sail   Black Sea   moon like you
rising out of bed   like you   brief as soldiers
Cybebe invading Rome   crazed mobs   plots
streets alleyways river Carthage again under
siege   salted by Rome   Remember Sicily   the shock
of history   how ghostly I feel   time   laid waste
burned   devotees unwelcome in Rome   senatorial
cabals tribunes plots Bacchus ecstasy blood spilled
glorious city   betrayed me   me   slow march   Lucius dead in Samos

Mark 14: 43-52

It is springtime. Gethsemane burns with a green fire.
His followers sleep, two snoring, one wheezing,
the youngest whimpering like a dog as it slumbers.
A gentle breeze chills the air with lingering
hints of an icy winter. The moon is white
and pocked as the bald pate of a Sadducee.
Gnats swarm over a thin pool of water gathered
from dew. After a long night's carousing,
serving feasting legionnaires, wearing no more
than a linen cloth as the centurion who hired
him demanded, a hungry boy picks a fig not yet
ripe or sweet enough to eat. One of twelve
lies prostrate but fully awake as he shifts
himself onto his knees and continues to pray.
Behind him, soldiers march up a hill, some
laughing, some playfully shaking their spears
like children until chastised by their commander.
Only hares and wolves, deserters, slaves, unruly
barbarians need fear their wrath. Yet at the first
signs of their approach an owl hoots, a jackal
yips, frogs croak huskily, lizards scurry over
weeds and twigs, bats flap more loudly
than a flock of birds flying, soaring westward,
tree limbs shake and leaves shudder as winds
surge before a storm, the sound of their feet
pounding on clay and rock awakening the sleepers.
The praying man stands up and oddly smiles.
A Judaean peasant dressed in shawl, tunic,
and sandals kisses him. Another frees his sword.
Tumult. Mayhem. What sense to make of it?
Is it abandonment? Dissolution? Betrayal
upon betrayal? The chaos despair lets loose?
To chase after the others, to save himself,

the boy—'neaniskos,' not precisely 'young man'—
strips off his linen garment—a 'sindon,' whatever
that word might mean, 'tunic,' 'shirt,' probably
not 'loincloth'—as if it were being ripped or torn
off him by a lusting soldier. As wounds shed blood,
Roman torches drip red sparks onto the ground.
Stark naked, the boy flees, runs, runs faster into
the cover of night, the darkness of Jesus and his story,
and disappears, vanishes for good, as if forever.
Who is he? Why did he irrupt into Mark's gospel
only to escape, leave it as a stranger might?
I intend no comparison, analogy, translation,
allegory, or myth. No similes or metaphors.
No blasphemy either, though I cherish the heresies
lives conspire with to tell their ordinary stories,
those that happen every day, nothing miraculous
about them. It is the enigma of why after
Jay died of a soft sarcoma, Bill from shooting
himself in the stomach, John by poisoning his body
with drugs, Luke from a car crash on 441,
so many friends lost to AIDS, too many to name,
the unseen many of history, why they abide,
why those that vanish from us stay after departure
not as ghosts, but lives unfinished at the end of it all.
I know what I claim in its strangeness makes no sense.
It is the inexplicable deep dark dwelling in things,
in moments, that holiness clings to like a lover
and will not let go. It is the mystery of joy's
sorrows, the ecstasy of the unknown torn from grief.
It is, yes, you, naked, unclothed, the night you
left me, this senseless semblance, the linen garment
you abandoned I hold now burning in my empty hands,
even that remnant of a life now departed bearing the sacredness of love.

Luke 24: 28-53

Then they neared the town to which they'd been
walking but, as they approached it, coming
much closer, he seemed to be leaving between
him and them a great distance. It was evening

when they saw him again, joining them at the table,
breaking the bread and blessing it before
he vanished more. Yet they felt at last capable
of better understanding him, the love they bore

for him and his for them made visible in the meal
they'd enjoyed together. And when he bared
his wounds, offered his flesh to them, to feel
and touch, they knew he was no mere spirit. They'd shared

their fish with him and seemed to comprehend what he'd meant.
They were his witnesses, clothed in his light, the friend sent
to them to bless them, comfort them as memory might do
when it offers to you its love, revealing its living wounds to heal you.

Seneca, Fragments from Agamemnon

First Chorister

As a man is, so he must do. What more can
humanity endure? A heart should break,
but cannot heal its pain during the span
of its lifetime, long or short. Awake,
asleep, outraged at the gods' lack of pity,
at how they torment mortals, let us mourn
the old frail man Priam whom, without mercy,
Pyrrhus slaughtered at Jupiter's altar, torn
from Hecuba's arms in the temple while she
prayed. Let the world be told her story,
why crazed by loss she came to see how
agony shoots inside you war's deadliest bows and arrows.

Second Chorister

We retain a foolish, lifelong attachment to
our bodies, those dust-bound corpses we
confound with our souls. Head to toe,
in our livers, hearts, lungs, bones, we
are sailors clinging to a storm-borne
ship as if to dear life. Even if the sea offers
us its spare freedom, though we've sworn
to endure all suffering no matter
what, beware of drowning in its other sorrows.
Death is a resentful monster. The gods are pitiless.
Agamemnon, be wary, too. There are no tomorrows.
You're sailing home mapless, unknowing, proud and reckless.

First Chorister

I watched as the sword glanced
and fell. There was a puddle
of blood beneath it as Electra danced
wildly after. Revenge is a riddle.
Who knows what's just? Agamemnon
old, blood-hunted, weary of war,
bored by sky and stars and sun,
driven by a fate destroying him far
from Troy. Some violence remains
in the minds of men forever, as if it explains
human suffering by the centuries
of cries passing its message from hearer to hearer:
Declaring all that began on Aulis when a king sacrificed
his daughter was owing to the whims of gods, ruthless and lawless.

Second Chorister

So history began, it's rumored. In time, treachery
turns on the king. Fair's fair.
His wife's betrayal. Her weak, petty
paramour's narrow conspiracy to dare
to slay him with an ax. My poor soul
trembles to speak of so brutal a moment,
the fear I see on his face as his whole
life wells up before him as if in testament
to its horrors, Snared, netted, trapped, then
enshrouded. How thin, precarious human skin
is. Whack, hack, slaughter mother, her lover.
too: at last it's over, Orestes. Dance on, Electra, maddened,
crazed, vengeful, snake-wreathed sister. Your mother
lies dead beside her lover under a sky wine-drunk, stoic, and sun-blinded.

Cassandra

Do not believe me. No one does. History ends here,
after it's barely begun. There's everything left to fear.
The dead alone comfort the dead, all surviving Trojans
widowed, enslaved, raped, driven mad, though the last
soldier's raid is over. Our queen crawls on the ground,
howls like a trapped wolf while reason embraces lies,
denies the truth. I am alone, though Apollo once loved
me, but the sun makes no attempt to cure my solitude.
Cold and parched and fickle, my lips tremble, my face
is pale and haggard, the few days left me destitute and hard.
Bleeding wounds, the clamor of metal on metal. Visions
returning, testifying to nothing, to no avail, the moans of those
dying in wars, the world's misery mirroring my grief and pain
like a twin standing behind me shadowed by history's stubborn remnants.

It suffices to tarry in life a few hours, then be gone.
Hector, Troilus, Deiphobus dead, dragged in the dirt,
carried, carted over into a darker, bleaker world.
If you should see what I saw or come to know what
I have known, you won't be able to forget
anything you've witnessed, must live it through
again and again with no one living believing you
or showing you mercy, no one listening to your story.
I feel sometimes like a woman lying on her deathbed
as if dying repeatedly every night, unable to let
her sorrows and regret go, but crying, weeping
over and over like me for my lost city, the burning
plains of Troy, its tombs and graves, its fields of the unburied
dead harkening to all I've prophesied, warned them about, too late and unheeded.

Excursus after the Play Is Over

And so his play in a way reverberates into
the ironic tragedies of history. A failing
moon looks veiled behind a parchment
page the soft light color of a calf's stretched
hide, beaten thin. What act can make
Rome more righteous? The Tiber's a gritty
gray seen by candlelight this late into
the night while he watches the full moon
decline, pale as the face of a helmsman
who once guided one of his ships in a storm,
saving them all. Nothing else is right, civility
doomed under his emperor. Loud as troops
marching at a steady pace, the river slaps
and sloshes on the hulls of docked boats. A few
stray clouds slip out of sight. An omen perhaps.
Every side now is his foe. He feels like an innocent
schoolboy reading about Cicero as he waits
in plain sight, his bald pate pallid from age,
not frightened by the feet he hears stomping
on his patio, Is this the summit of stoicism,
to die unafraid? A citizen of Rome must speak
his mind freely, despite the risks. Yet how
grimly this night tests him. And so Seneca
calmly closes his curtains, and, as Nero has told
him he must, checks the bath water to see if it is
hot enough, his knife razor sharp and silvery by moonlight.

Gods, after Friedrich Hölderlin

1.

Holy Socrates, why do you ceaselessly give yourself
    to that young man? Are you not concerned with
      loftier matters? Why do you stare at him
        so longingly, with the love owed to gods?

Those who think most profoundly love what's most vital.
    Those who see the world clearly admire youth's splendor.
    Those who are wisest will, at last,
      worship whatever is most beautiful.

2.

Their quieted hearts were filled with a silent contentment
 and, as from the beginning, alone, desire was satisfied.
Such is man, if fortune is true and he is granted its gifts
 by a god, though he sees and understands none of it.
First he must suffer. For now he names the beloved things.
 Now he must pursue the words that bud and blossom like flowers.

3.

Sacred realm of the Greeks, home to the gods,
 is it true, what youth taught us?
Hall of feasts, its floor the sea whose tables are mountains
 built in a holier time to fulfill a great need!
But where are the thrones, where the temples, their vessels?
 Where the songs that please the gods like nectar?
Where, oh where do they shine, the oracular truths?
 Delphi slumbers. Where now does tragedy sing?

Where is quickness? Where does one see omnipotent joy
 break out of the sky to dazzle eyes, ravage ears with thunder?
Father Aether! Someone cried and voice after voice took up
 the chant a thousand times and more. Who can bear life alone?
Shared fortune proffers joy. And, later, with strangers exchanged,
 it yields an exultation, words, words as exalted as sleep.

Father! Oh mind-piercing clarities. How far they travel. An ancient
 sign passed down, now distant, yet striking, penetrating, creating
what paradise has given. As heaven enters, its presence shakes the earth
 awake from its shadows and man from his gloom strides into Day.

After Friedrich Hölderlin and Johann Jacobi: A Child's Wilderness

1.

When I was a child, I thought like a child,
wandering in forests, alone, free,
unseen, hugging trees, one with the wild
wooded things growing inside me
I'd hike through nightly in dreams. Old, I'd like
to tell you stories of harmony and joy,
but I fear, now, they might strike
you as folly. I was still a mere boy
when the knowledge of death fell
upon me, dimming the sun. If deities
set the world, by a magical spell,
into order once, it's fallen to pieces
since. Is it childish now, out of hopelessness,
to pray, to beg ancient places to return, to save us?

2.

Father, Mother, someone outside
cried. I heard. Yet another voice
took up the chant.
Who can bear life alone?
Father, Mother, passing
on their clarities, a sign
that life has meaning
beyond what's already given
you to know on your own,
as if the earth were shaken
awake by understanding the choice
is not yours only but that of those who've died
before you, welcoming you back home,
believing what you, without them, never could and can't.

3.

The woods' heart is quieted,
filled with contentment
when time is satisfied.
That is why it must be silent.
It will bear no trace I was there,
that I'd ever wandered through
it freely, breathed its air,
risked getting lost daring new
ways to explore it, wanting to suffer
its darkness alone, though frightened by
the unknown ways and all that's scary
in the wild places of late night,
unable so sleep, yet too much the dreamer,
with the fire's last flames burning into my sight.

4.

May all souls rest in peace,
their suffering over,
their pain ended.
It is time to cease
dreaming, life briefer
than a flame, extinguished
by winds. You who rejoiced in the sun,
wandered often under the moon,
will return to the woods soon
now your life is done.
And those you love
may they walk with you above
the tree line to see the world you've left as heaven
sees it, as it was when given us at the first creation.

Théophile Gautier, L'Art

It's so. For art to be beautiful
it must be difficult to do.
It must rebel against you,
like onyx, marble, enamel.

It must resist you, like the shoes
that heighten the stature
of a masked tragic actor
in Greece, inspired by the muses.

Eschew slack rhythms. Bring
back the strictures of shoes
tightly fit for working
hardest, though painful to use.

Sculptor. If the clay you sculpt
with yields to your fingers
easily, pliably, the result
denies the mind its urge to linger.

See how a trinitarian halo
forms a globe below
a cross, like a sign of eternality,
over Jesus and Mary?

All things pass away, yet
a bronze bust survives
a fallen city. Set
art apart. It lives. It thrives.

Even the gods die. But as Horace
wrote, poetry, if formal,
imperial always wins first place
against bronze statuary, its only rival.

Chisel, file, sand, carve, mould.
All art aspires to sculpture.
The enduring dream, the rapture
of an aspiring life that never grows old.

Théodore de Banville, Nous n'irons plus au bois...

We'll go to the woods no more now the oak
and laurel have been axed down. Were there
nymphs and naiads swimming in the lake,
cupids hiding among trees, a scurrying pair
of fauns racing from a centaur through a meadow
when we were young? The sun, when it struck
waves, bounced off stones, joined the flow
of creeks and streams, turned crystalline. Luck
can be like that in childhood. You can hear the sound
of horns, the hooves of a stag running through brush,
the peeling of bells from a castle's tower bewitching
children happily lost in wilderness. Now, instead, all around
you you hear only the noise of chopping, cutting, scything.
No more skittering squirrels. No more deities. No songs of the thrush.

Gérard de Nerval, Myrtho

I think of you often, wise, sacred magician, enchanting
Myrtho, from bold Posillipo, its volcano always on fire
near the bay of Naples, its flames perpetually bursting
skyward, your face immortally ablaze with the radiance of desire,

like queens of the East, the gold of their braids mingled
with the black of the darkest purple grapes. I first tasted
drunkenness from your cup, from how your eyes had smiled,
flashing at me. I felt I was praying at his feet while Bacchus said,

like a muse inspiring me, I was one of Greece's chosen sons. I know
why Vesuvius is exploding again, Myrtho. You touched, grazed
it gently with your feet and suddenly, like a field you'd sow
with seed, it grew dark with ash and the whole bay sooty and hazed-

in. I know too why a Norman duke broke your iconic, sacred
gods moulded from clay since ever since he did so the bay
of Naples, Virgil's holy bay, lets grow the pale, northern-bred
hydrangeas and its own lushly green myrtles as one, to celebrate each day.

Gérard de Nerval, El Desdichado

I am the shadowy man, the widower, the disconsolate
Prince of Aquitaine who resides in his ruined tower.
My only star has died. My guitar's starry strings dictate
I play solely the notes of Melancholia's black sun. The hour

has come, the night of the tomb. You, who consoled me, take
me back to Posillipo, the sea's stairway, the Italian
flowers that soothed my heart, the arbor, to make
me happy again, whose vines, roses entwined as one.

Am I love? Or am I Phoebus Apollo? King of Jerusalem
or that adventurous lover, the Duke of Biron? My face
still burns from traces of your kisses, my Bethlehem
star, my queen. I dream of sirens swimming freely in a place

like a grotto, a song-filled sea-cave. Like Aeneas, Dante,
I have crossed the Acheron without having died yet,
playing Orpheus's lyre, the one I strum to write my poetry,
greeting this saint or that, listening to fairies' sighs where no stars set.

Arthur Rimbaud, L'éternité

Discovered again.
What? Eternity,
the light of the sun
become sea.

Watchman of the soul,
never tire
of quietly saying, Night is nothing,
the day on fire.

From the world's approval,
from vulgar high-
spirits, remove
yourself, fly freely.

Then, from you alone,
you, your glowing satin ashes,
duty breathes easily, though stone
silent. No one says, No more,

there is no hope. All is done.
No 'orietur.' Nothing stirs. Nothing rises.
Knowledge comes from patience.
No suffering you feel, no pain surprises.

Recovered, renewed again.
What is? Eternity.
The light of the sun's
become sea.

After Passages in Poems by Georg Trakl

1.

The grapes in the crystal bowl are blue-black as bruises.
The tallest trees, toppling, crack louder than gun shots.
"The days ahead are terrifying." So the sun says,
brightening. Read omens. Close doors, windows. Cast lots.

The eastern hills are golden, ripe for freshly burning.
An effigy made from corn husk is set on fire in a rite
of late life. A man you know is falling, falling, falling,
without ever landing on earth, out of reach, out of sight.

The air is febrile, tasteless, with a new transparency.
What can you not see more clearly by breathing it?
You walk beneath an ageless sky as if you were free,
as if dawn's clarity were a savage lover you've submitted to.

2.

An autumn sun in late summer, leaves falling
from trees, brittle, sly, and unpredictable,
the spaces around them shyly sighing.
It is a hot afternoon, with no place left for people.

The air tastes of metal and something
white and unpalatable. An absent-minded
dune drifts east. A young girl begins to sing
of better times than these too bright ones in the present.

She likes to believe the many-hued colors of the sea
are the colors of God. Maybe she's right.
Shadows twist on the hills behind where we
stand, their dark furrows restless as sleepers on a blistering night.

Sunset descends: the red of wine in fluted glasses, embers
burning slowly out, drifting logs from nearby forests,
dreams of recollected violence. Its silence is also hers,
the young girl's—too awed to sing on—and God's reign here, and August's.

3.

Melancholia keeps returning, insistent
as loneliness, yet gentle as the saddest
Schubert lied. It feels, sometimes, heaven-sent,

painful in the way humanity suffers
most keenly when happiness is no longer
possible, nor peace. These days are dark waters

and turbulent seas. A dying man grieves
and you grieve for him to please

the sky, the stars, the moon as it wanders while the man
lowers his head onto a pillow, somnolent, yet restless.

After Two Librettos by Hugo von Hoffmansthal

1. The Marschallin

What fate chooses what death should be ours
since, despite our pleas, it always takes us sooner
or later? Time both nourishes and devours
us as it pleases. To the young it doesn't matter
much. Older, we dread it daily. Look at your face,
the marks of age on it. See how every mirror
repeats the common story. You can feel it, trace
it racing through your veins like blood. Like sand
in an hour glass, life pours slowly, silently out.
Sometimes in the darkest hours I take your hand
and stalk the corridors of our old house as if I'm about
to understand our lives at last by stopping all the clocks
in every room, by covering every surviving looking glass.
Tick-tocks, chiming bells, each breath, each second unlocks
another mystery. I listen as he kisses me and let him pass.
Lightly, lightly time races by so fast you can see it going, leaving
you behind. Lightly, lightly you must follow even as the bells are chiming.

2. Ariadne

There is a stranger's empire where all is purity,
called the land of death. Here, where we
now live, nothing is innocent. A wand-bearer,
glorious as Hermes, with his sandals' wings,
will descend to me and in his arms gather
me up to him. Imagine his dreadful beauty.
Imagine his serenity, how he sings and sings
against loss and grief and perpetual sorrow.
I will hear his footsteps approaching my cave.
I will hear his voice as he reaches me ever
nearer. He will touch my heart, cover

my eyes, a god too blinding to look upon save
with the purest, mute adoration. I will borrow
my mother's most festive robes and rings to wear.
Light leaves in breezes will waft down gently
before us, happily falling. I will be darkness. I will be
incorporeal, freed from the burden of being alive to offer
myself completely to him, this bitter thing I was, this Ariadne,
transfigured into song by my savior, music's blessèd, wingèd messenger.

III
Remainders

Hay and Wicker Man

His face is a mask of white muslin gauze stretched
on his skull. Fox and bear used to waltz together
in these woods, he tells me, where quail, red tail deer
wandered as freely. He brings me things he has fetched

from thickets and undergrowth for me to keep
stored in a box safe as jewels–plain bird feathers,
lizards' bones, claw-shaped roots to help me sleep,
dreams to gnaw on when I'm hungry, pelts and furs

of dead mammals he gathers to warm my bed at night.
Trees can't lie, he says, nor winds tell falsehoods.
The moon is a raven's eye that never dares blink
though the sun rises late. He says: Hold me tight

to your grief and sorrows, to the oughts and shoulds
you sought to live up to and failed to follow. Think
of all the times you sought to confess the truth
but couldn't, the liar you became of your later youth.

Now, you've no more more childhood left to bury.
You'll dig your grave soon beneath moss-soft forest
sod. Keep faith in God, in eternity, while your body
leaves you prey to the pain that has never let you rest

all your long life. An autumn chill blows from the east

off the sea, westward down mountains.   My dear,

I do not mean to scare you. I am no ravaging beast

seeking to devour your sleep. I am the twin you fear

who stole his ghost face from a hawk's breast, from thorn

wood, white and sallow. The end is forever beginning.

Have I not sworn to keep true, never to mourn

you, to stay with you always, we two always one, never parting?

Free Variations on an Ancient Theme

Moments ago, Dawn, rising golden-sandled,
shone through the trellis of my room....

Sometimes at sunset the moon is also
rosy-fingered, more beautiful than the stars.
And her light, her pale clear light
Illuminates both seas and wild fields
full of new flowers alike....

                Sappho

1.

The penumbral late night sky is tinted blue
with picture-still, iron gray, ashen
clouds floating above a coal-black,
miles-long cloud that stretches across
the heavens like a huge banner hung in mourning.

In the distance, a cruise ship, its lights
on, lively as a city's, lingers
on the horizon, waiting
until dawn to sail into the bay.
The full moon sweeps a broad trail

of bright sparkling light over an ocean
that's quiet as a lake, an ultramarine
so deep it looks like black ink, like stone
stele in a museum, glistening under
skylights the moon's rays softly pour through.

Northward, near the headlands, a cargo ship
heads west as the moon drifts down
into the ominous cloud that hides its light,
then slowly slips below it, hovering over the earth
like the balloon in Rousseau's View of Clichy Bridge at Asnières.

2.

A brisk, crackling late night wind blows
during a sunrise whose golden-
red rays arc in halos

over the hills, turning the ocean
into a burning field
seen from an airplane,

the beach amber, the waves' crests
coppery, the night-black ravens
a tarnished bronze.

Gliding over the cliffs inspired by
the light, gulls fly
higher, then vanish where

trees cast dark shadows, the sun
like a torch leading them
to the cliffs where they feed.

3.

A brisk, cool wind during a sunset
gilding, brightening sparrows'
feathers to an opalescent gleam,

the bluffs blazing, the sandstone
cliffs like yellow jade,
the sea green and gray

and blue as a peacock's tail,
the beach cinnamon-
brown, like glimmering oiled raw hide,

the ice plants the green of
tarnished copper,
their petals rose, lavender, pink:

imagine this moment is the light shining
through Our Lady of Chartres
Cathedral's stained glass windows

as you sat near the altar listening to a boys'
choir in a loft high above you,
singing a mass in praise of God by Josquin des Prez.

4.

While the tide is shifting, wait
as a docked boat waits
to return to sea,

the sun hesitating, too, as if it
is waiting
for the tide to go out,

since waves now batter a beach
too risky to walk
beside safely for fear

of rogue waves. The old ways
of believing are over.
Soon the moon, not the sun,

will shine over the ocean
for no other reason
than how like it is as it changes.

5.

A breathless November evening near sunset.
A path slopes down to a shallow, mossy
creek. Denuded trees' branches form a net
like a spider's web threaded against the sky.

The sun becomes invisible beyond the thicket
of limbs and spiky pine needles, its last
light filtered by woods as it grows, like regret,
slowly dimmer until it's almost forgotten, sinking fast.

Yellow, orange, blood red, then a somber fiery
maroon, the sun's light quickly vanishes into
night, the day's few traces lost to visibility,
no longer retrievable. What else is there to know?

6.

The dark deep in woods is lonely. Yet a heron is awake,
wading in the lake where mallards, plump, tame
geese sleep among reeds while a solitary king snake
slips into waters over which fireflies flicker like a candle's flame.

7.

Scattered clouds. Arched, scimitar-sharp,
a new moon rises over the sea
while an old man strolls alone on the beach
in no rush, keeping watch for a while.
A boat, tossed by gusts, is warping
against the wind, no longer free,
tied to a sea-anchor, breaching
the calm until it's safer to sail out.
The old, tired man stands on the shore,
leaning on a pole for support, the crane of
his heart soaring to the moon, lost in its light.

8.

Time is never confessional. It's about
sunset, the smell of smoke
from burning leaves in autumn

without remorse or nostalgia,
evening's final
traces fading into night.

It is about following a creak to a lake
where the moon shines for no one's
sake on water so calm

not even a boy wading in
can disturb it, floating
in it happily while his spirit drifts

further into night, suspended, constant
as star, timeless as a prayer
left unanswered.

9.

A pelican, a hawk, a raven
rest on a rail in a tight row,
stone rigid, claws hidden
by clumps of seagrass that grow

from mounds of sand piled on
the holiday-closed highway:
a trio of birds, as the sun
weakens, staring beyond the bay

past the last of sunset to the light
of morning
despite the oncoming night,
as if daring

the dark to scare them, three birds waiting for day-
break, to fly
toward its light, too high
to reach, too far away.

Two Tragic Figures

"Es sei nicht immer Tag und auch nicht Nacht."
(It is not always day nor is it night.)
    Friedrich Hölderlin, *Empédocles*

1. Young Oedipus

He dreams of his father coming at him in
the attic of the palace with knife in hand
and of a wife whose eyes in a mirror
cause it to break into tears like hers.

Tempted by an abyss like the comforts
of bed, he slips out of sight, can't understand
what his name augurs, why his foot swells,
why his easy youth is filled with fears.

He picks up children in his arms. Holds
them. Loves them as he does the mother
he embraces. A blind man lurks in his sleep,
his beard spittle gray. He lies to him. Swears

he never trips when he is constantly falling.
He loses every race he runs in. The old
women in the plaza weep. Speak to him
the name of a strange city. Then pray.

In the mornings, words spill from his mouth
on their own, like a great king's without
thinking. As he bathes, his nakedness
shines like a god become human.

His father praises his eloquence. A boy,
he says, is a seed the gods have sewn.
Pain is destined. Rage against it reverently.
A dark grove calls you. Be led to it by silence.

2. *Betrayed Clytemnestra*

A narrow palace, ghost-haunted
halls, stone walls, iron gates,
gold masks, bronze doors,
cliffs behind it pouring water

off rock morning cold and frost-
colored, a marble fountain
bearing water from the sacred
mountain, its hillsides hiding

in its leaves, vines, and outcrops
the spirits of soldiers who died
in battle. Her husband will die
too, for lying to her, not defying

the gods. Last night, she dreamed
of a coiled snake she tried
to feed with her breast. It bit
her and curdled her milk. Her son.

Her sole son will return after it's done
with his strong sword. Let it come true,
her serpentine, ophidian dream
of dying by her love for her boy,

since her screams that day will awaken
her sleeping guards, her cries'
auspicious as hawks', summoning
the furies of guilt to pursue him forever.

Scandinavia

to the music of Allan Pettersson

Call it Norway or maybe Sweden, or any other place
as cold, the saga-laden world he yearns to die
in, the icy peaks, fjords, birch woods he'd left no trace
in of himself. Yet far north was who he was, why
he could never say. Let a bitter wind blow over
the tundra. Snow is what his life has meant,
the strange chill of age that began the moment
he was born, a January frost in all he's known or loved,
his life like a statue chiseled from a block of ice: that
crystalline, that splendid, like what he felt when moved
by passion: the clean, new fallen snow reflecting the sun
on a clear morning, its bright, bleak world his true habitat.
the blinding glare he'd seen it by like the meaning of anything done,
accomplished heading, now it's ended, toward the peace of a final winter.

Gundula Janowitz Singing Strauss' Four Last Songs

Return to a lost world on a wild, windy, rainy night.

Trust in first things, the loamy, sopping earth

steaming in the heat of morning, the half-light

of clouds in a stormy summer sky, the rebirth

of wonder in the quiet of woods smelling of sod,

oak roots, spruce, pine needles, drenched brush.

A stream cut from rock by cascading waterfalls

rushes on. Petals and leaves swirl in froth. Prod

under a rock, find beetles and worms and odd

pale twigs twisted in knots. A weedy path calls

back to you in the aftermath of tragedy. Sweaty

bark fragrant with resin, dense, minty vines in woods

that lure you ever deeper in but will not let you stay

there where your life belongs not to you alone but, from faraway,

to the voice you hear as, lying by a creek, you sink into sleep, rapt by its beauty.

The End to the War in the East

1.

Because he didn't see or hear it, the child
he was then swore it could not have happened.
He was too young and never had been exposed
to the photos of the cloud, the city after
its incineration, the charred, peeling bodies
lying among ashes. How could he guess
the world before that moment would never
return? That there exist cruelties that are
unforgivable no matter how some might try
to excuse them? to justify the faceless dead
floating in the midst of ruin in the Motoyasu River?

Yet, seeing the images years later, he knew
those times were when the nightmare began,
a seizure of the spirit unsparing
in its capacity to terrify, to incite
a dread that descends upon men,
women, children alike when faced
with the cruel, brute realities of bombing
anything because no one is ever young, safe,
or innocent enough to find release
from their participation in it whenever
terror is waged in their names for the sake of peace.

2.

Pearl is burning, on and on. As Saipan's plains burn. Civilians
hide in caves, shooting, strangling their children,
then leaping from cliffs, innocents, the thousands
dying in mass suicides; burns on the day when
General Saito proclaims to his men, "In death there is life,"

and, with his ceremonial sword, commits seppuku
as an adjutant shoots him; burns, by bullet and knife,
when an officer kills his men, beheading them who
began to die when their Zeros bombed Pearl. It is the way
of wars never to end. No soldier can ever really surrender.
The men struck at dawn at Pearl or under the midday
glare on the Bataan road are there, in memory, for the slaughter
over and over. To promise them peace is a lie. Violence is prophecy.
Pearl burns. Tokyo burns. Okinawa. Now as then. Unceasing. Nagasaki.

Orlando

This is some of what he remembers best. His face
staring back at him in the mirror as he shaved
The way he held his fork and knife as he ate, relishing
each bite. His wavy black hair, brown eyes flecked with copper.

His lithe body as he danced, twirling, whirling in place.
How he kissed him, cared for him, held him, saved
him from his wounds. How he twitched, moaned making
love, how sweetly he smiled after. The way he ran, would race

him home after the bars had closed. The time he waved
at him from across the room when they first met, already his lover,
who is loss now and grief and the senselessness of it
and a mourning that no one must ever try to leave behind or forget or quit.

Son Frère

after the film by Philippe Besson and François Ozon

A boat in harbor is waiting for
the tide to change, eager
to return to the ocean.

Tonight, it's is too wild, free
to risk standing near
its fiercest waves.

Whatever strife troubles your life
belongs to the lost faith
of believing in gods.

Don't leave us. Don't go. What are
you yearning to know from
dying that's new?

The moon has chosen to shine on the ocean
to learn why it changes like it,
though men don't.

Your haunted dark eyes leave nothing for sight
to bind to, the bright bravery
of blindness.

If you are hoping for someone to come
this late in the evening
to save you,

it will be yourself reborn in my mirror, the one
I use to shave by, looking for you
over my shoulder.

Black night, shimmering clouds,
rolling waves: the sea's
mercilessness

to the ones it's exiled are ours
to each other,
brother.

Oar and Cross

At home with his wife and son after twenty
years apart at war and the fateful, arduous
journey back, fraught with dangers—a hostile sea,
the sorrows of the dead, brutal, monstrous
men and creatures, the caves of a Demi-goddess—
Odysseus grows restless, leaves a goodbye note
on their kitchen table, and sets forth to free
himself from purpose, rules, laws, eager to devote
what remains of his days to wandering, planting a last oar
in a desolate desert, then walking nowhere, alone, aimless,
naked, wondering what his life meant to the gods, what it's been for.

After his death, brief entombment, and surprising,
stupefying resurrection, enjoying what
his followers designated a picnic (he need bring
only himself, they said), the morning bright and hot,
the sea salty sweet and lovely, not at all stormy,
he prefers to walk alone, mystified that he's not
content, not happy, but near despair, his body,
spirit still suffering despite the glory they shine on
the earth now, on each friend, passerby, companion
he speaks to. Yet he wonders why it was lives like theirs he forgot
to live since there was so much no god could understand about
people since, though like them he'd been forsaken and known doubt,
his body had never been corrupted by worms and time and the horrors of rot.

Aesop

This morning, early, I watched a hungry crow
carefully examine an indented, bent, but sturdy
plastic food container with almost no
food left in it a likely passing driver had carelessly
tossed out of a car window onto the street.
Peck. Peck. Peck. The crow's beak
as it worked sounded like the steady beat
of a hammer against tin. Peck. Peck. Peck.
I considered trying a human intervention by
removing the cover for it, but it was too filthy
with crud to handle. Peck. Peck. It took ten
minutes at least for it to begin to break through
the lid and eat the two bits of gray meat left. When
it had finished, cawing, hungry, wanting more, it flew
high off and far away, refuting patience as the moral of its story.

An Abandoned House

A spindle back chair made from black
walnut. Embroidered, plump red
pillows faded to rose, a pale
olive sweater draped over a stool.
Swinging freely, the door to the shack
creaks like floor boards in the shed
behind the barn. A harness for a mule
hangs on a wall hook by a rusty nail.
Heavy work boots rest under a bed.
A hutch, with thick slats, displays
pewter cups and ceramic plates
and bowls. A calendar with no days
marked or circled on it lies open
on a table to December. A shovel waits,
propped against a bin, for someone
to clear the walkway from a night's heavy
snowfall. An ironing board uneasily
dangles from its peg. Lonely things,
mourning for what never comes back,
for how long they've been left forgotten.

By the river, a hickory and oak grove surrounds
a cemetery whose dead have been left alone,
too, ever since the last of their family
vanished, who knows why? A few tattered,
faded, century old flags flap from corroded
poles whenever strong winds blow through.
Empty of human presence, the mossy tombstones
go untended, left to crack, entangled by ivy
and brush, history forsaken in the angry,
abandoned, silenced farmland of Washington County.

Of the Farm

to the memory of D. S. Carne-Ross

Late summer. A small wheat field. Woods near by,
hickory, oak, sycamore. He's harvesting grain
the old way, the ancient way, with hand and scythe.
Each new sheaf he binds elates him. The wain
is piled high. Massive clouds billow. A shower
or two will follow soon, like the sureties of home
once the wheat is gathered in. Crocuses, asters,
gentiana, lilies blossom near him, sweet as the loam
he plows each spring alone. Let his life end like a sunset
that comes so quickly its fires entwine trees and brush
and him together. It is the time for burning of the chaff, wet
or dry, consumed by a blaze whose veils of smoke will rush
skyward as the burnt stalks, leaves, kernels, saved seeds
become a mother's re-risen child, a revelation of poetry and its poet,
of what both can be if you till its language and all its mortal matter
with the devotion owed to the undying earth, Demeter and her daughter.

Massachusetts

A squall is swelling over its woods. The sassafras smells
bitter. Billowing winds strip trees of their last leaves
(rust, scarlet, gold) twist weeds, bend reeds, scatter shells
and pebbles along rocky banks. Like a vast beast, day heaves

itself awake, frightened by the gathering storm as the sky
ripples like dancing ribbons of watery blue, stone gray,
ebony, colors the lake reflects and mimics. Clouds race by
like wisps of mist obscuring the tree line. Bushes, shrubs sway

with the shifting currents, bow without breaking, shudder
at the thunder as it reverberates off the mountain.
There's a naked man adrift in the lake, a rower
without oars, bone-cold and wet, who seems uncertain

of how or whether he'll ever be borne back to shore since winter
came early to claim for itself the splendors of western
waters and forests at the peak of autumn, the storm
blowing harder as his rowboat floats, circling in harm's

way while a fierce gust topples an oak that cracks as scarily
as lightning until it sinks beneath the lapping water where
its leafless branches and mossy trunk disappear,
slowly slipping onto the lake's deep bed, soft as silt, yet muddy.

Water is what I mean when I speak of despair since a lake, like regrets,
is made from the same stuff as the stormy sky, and sleep is where
thunder rumbles loudest, winds howl most deafeningly for the sole sake
of waking you while you dream of a man floating in a rowboat happily

alone in western Massachusetts.

Shannon's Suicide

1.

A Southern night. Fireflies. A quiet sky.
Cattle roaming the pasture. Stars lit
bright enough to see by. Fingers gently
caressing each other's faces. Why
not kiss? How to make its pieces fit
together like parts of a puzzle? Memory
never suffices. There is where I'd begin
again. In the midnight silence of a lake.
A slow creek flowing over a low stone dam.
Jasmine, magnolia in the air. Sweaty skin.
Breathless sighs. Closed eyes. For the sake
of the past, I rely on the magic bestowed on
matter by imagination, bodies transfigured by
desire. As if time should prove good, what can
be imagined made visible, love renewed by resurrection.

2.

Without succession, day follows day, the hours sleep
like boys along a stream. Dawn's a snake sunning
its back, flickering its tongue, its dusky tail. Deep
into dream-life, so it goes. The two of us hiking

in woods, in honeysuckle summer. Imagine a catch
in the breath that lasts for years, this young heart,
these old tears, a shack, its shingle roof, broken latch,
the uninhabited places no one alive belongs to, is part

of anymore where a naked boy stands in a wide creek
who seems to have stepped out of the cliff behind
him, lost forest voices confusing choices, what to seek
from backward glances, reminiscences, what's left to find

in the sheen of light piercing the canopy like a word half-heard
or memory uncertain of what is conceivable if everything's blurred.

3.
Dozers, dump trucks, road wideners,
back hoes, milling machine, asphalt pavers,
filing cabinets too, typewriters, his father's
roll top oak desk, all sold at court-ordered

auction, patrimony lost, his brother
ruined as he is, both divorced: apart,
happier, Shannon's wife's a success at
her dress shop catering to the stylish few.

Self-exiled along the New River,
redneck's shack all he can afford,
crumbling pier, unstable dock,
his twenty year old prized boat

we used to sail in anchored there
until one night, south of Wrightsville,
he takes the rot-gutted boat out
thrilling to how the winds make steering

it rough as he waits for the time
to scuttle it with hatchet, ax,
drill,
augur.

A Gas Station in Western Guilford County, 1956

A farmer's faded bib overalls are spattered with red clay,
his face, neck, and hands cracked, scabbed, and ruddy,
his clothes sweat-soaked as he eats pimento cheese, jelly
sandwiches by the gas station's pumps. The day
is too hot for shade to cool anyone. A dog with ticks
scratches behind the cola cooler, yelps, licks a bone. A truck
stops to refuel, its bed loaded with lumber and bricks.
A battered Buick's on the mechanic's lift. To make a buck
or two, three teenaged boys wait for a pick-up to come
to take them to the tobacco fields for work. It's early
in the morning at the start of July with its steady hum
of locusts, chirping crickets, birds. Is this the future the boy sees
as he sips his RC from a frosty bottle? A storage bin, a snuff rack, a drum
for drained oil, himself among those silent men, these shadeless ancient trees?

Afire

1.

Craggy mountains shadow a sleeping city, their peaks
singed by last month's fires. A few spindly, drab
trees survive on western flanks. The air still reeks
of smoke. The stars are invisible, the sky scab
black, streaked with red. It is a time without season,
the earth numb from its need for sleep. In the west,
far from here, fires are still being fought. Reason
is any night one wanders far off in search of rest.
A lake that ash has settled on glows blue-white under
a full moon that spins in the heavens like the eye
of God. Go in fear of wolves, warthogs ravaging the land for
something to eat. Suppose humanity itself were a lie
we tell each other to stay hopeful, to bear the terror
of what we have done to air and earth and sky and water?

2.

Sunsets are scorched orange, every moon
is scarlet after so many years without
rain or peace. Soon, the soldiers say, soon
a great torrent will fall to end the drought
to quench earth's thirst. Slips of clouds float
through the sky like slivers of smoke
from unceasing fires. Wars have become rote,
like a dull job or love made too often. They choke
on their own breath, hunger after bread, a stew to eat,
beer to drink. Picture the emptiness
they sense being unable to tell what is real,
what is not, the gaping pits in streets,
the burned-out houses, blackened bodies. Feel
what they feel. The world's afire. And you its last witness.

Two of the Unchosen

1. Jonathan, Son of Saul

Sorely famished, he unknowingly disobeyed his father
by dipping his soldier's staff deep into a forest's floor
seeping with honey, eating despite the king's order
for his men to take no nourishment by day before
victory was theirs. He sipped the sticky honey spread
in golden pools thick as butter, not slowly dripped
from combs but spilled like wine gone straight to his head
the instant he ate it, all his appetite's doubts stripped
from eyes made keener by what he'd devoured. And so
he must die that night, his life condemned by a father's vow
to slaughter those who fed their hunger, failure to know
the law no excuse. But friends, faithful comrades, wouldn't allow
it, threatening rebellion, imploring, as a lover might have sung
to him, how sweet it was to taste, how sensual, how golden on the tongue.

And it came to pass in a time of the nation's desolation
that his father falls from favor, half-mad, having lost the power
he'd had over his people, his many wives, and Jonathan, the son
who'd disobeyed him and was no longer chosen. The Witch of Endor
rises out of the cave of his growing terror from whose words he
hears his doleful fate and so demands his son choose between lover
and him in the catastrophic civil war that is sure to come as swiftly
as his father's hatred toward him came after he'd seen his son's hunger
for dates and figs, honey and wine, satisfied where he lay in bed
naked, sung to by the man who would defeat him, always greedy
for more in his ambitious, libidinous manner: this upstate, usurper David,
a sweet singer, yes, but an even subtler liar.
                              But, Saul, don't you see,
now that you're dead, how he weeps for you and your boy, for, surpassing
the love of women, the love he felt for your son whom you made die for nothing?

2. Caliban

Solitude made the world but left undivided.   This
light and dark. Last night, I watched
a ground-hugging fog swallow a white-washed.
moon, famished for its light. My mother   thing
is Sycorax, witch and ironic comic. Am I
more night or day? I imagine Prospero dead
yet performing his magic tricks on and on.   of
I believe art begins, ends in lies and betrayals.
How else has he freed himself from my island
and Ariel so easily from his a tree and not me?   darkness
I dream. I dream every moment of beauty.
And I wake from each dream with heartache as I
look at my body. My master hit, tied, chastised   I
me for my attempts at usurpation. I would rebel
again and again from his infliction of pain on me,
yet how could I possibly abandon my island where   acknowledge
I endlessly dream of a world just like this one, only
better, and I no more a servant, a son but a dreamer
of sounds, sweet airs, voices that wake me and are   mine.

Two by Igor Stravinsky

1. *Orpheus*

"A long sustained slow chant," Stravinsky said
of his score. Instead of a lyre, a harp is played
over winds' sonorities in the land of the dead.
A walking bass line, precise rhythms, a parade
of musical, crystalline colors. Near the ballet's end,
the strings intone a mournful "sul ponticello"
to sing of serious things until, as Orpheus ascends
toward apotheosis, the horns play a fugue, slow
and solemn as a liturgy. "We live in the same
moment forever," Balanchine remarked. "There
is no future, no past." Death is not to blame
for enticing Orpheus into Hades. As they begin their
descent, they dance a pas de deux like lovers,
Thanatos and Eros, each body strong, taut as the other's.
All lost times are present once we've begun that dance
to the underworld to rescue the Eurydices we'll lose at a glance.

2. *Canticum Sacrum*

The light of stars is like the lamps lit
by wise virgins who had saved
enough oil for the bridegroom.
When he arrived after nightfall,
their wicks still burned.

Sit

with me. Listen. His music is being played
in San Marco's in the evening gloom
under Byzantine domes, mosaics and gold

near a lapping canal.

Or so I imagine: the chorus' voices transporting his body
on a flower-draped gondola
over lagoons, by the sea
to San Michele
as close to La Serenissima
as he is to God, lying under cypresses' funereal beauty.

Dawn's mist vanishes over the Lido.
Ships' flags
flap on a breezy
noon as a red-throated loon zigzags
over the piazza, San Marco,
all of Venice, crowned
by the sun at its zenith, like the carved marble sound
of his music, its vaulting naves, domes, bell towers,
or, in Cannaregio,
the clarity of the lions' mouths spouting waters
into the basin below.

Wander with me through San Michele as we contemplate the silent canticle
of the plain flat stone marking the grave of Igor Stravinsky.

Snowy Plovers

The windows of the houses on the Richmond Hills
appear to brighten simultaneously, like streetlights,
switched on all at once. Their moon-soft glow spills

over tree tops trembling in the breeze onto the heights
of the buildings below. Like a long, narrow swatch
of silk, orange-red and shiny, the last of sunset

stretches over the horizon, wet, bleeding into the sea.
I stand at water's edge as darkness gathers and watch
the snowy plovers–small, weightless as puff balls, jet

black in the night–scurry back and forth, almost nervously
as waves rush in and retreat leaving behind the tiny
crustaceans and worms they eat, so light on their feet

they seem to be gliding on the frothy film of water
the ocean sheds on the sand. There are hundreds of them,
flock after flock, steadily moving northward, one after

the other, taking flight only if frightened by a barking
dog or a child's clapping or squeal or sudden laughter
at seeing them, surprising them in the night. It is like a hymn,

I think: how, when they fly they rise no higher than a foot
or two above the beach, swirling together, a black whirling
flock of plovers nearly surrounding me like a smoky cloud,

then landing, en masse, a few yards north to feed some more
on the minuscule creatures the tide brings in. How to put
this? I stand alone, in an unknown sorrow, by ocean's edge,

sunset over, the ensuing darkness like someone's crying aloud
into infinity, as a man might hesitate on an upper ledge
of a high-rise enticed by the beauty he sees spread out

so freely before him, the unbearable sweetness of life like
the roar of the sea calling to him, Come. Come to me. I will restore
all you have lost. Everything. No need to delay. No need to doubt.

Leap. Jump in. The sea and its restless waves are waiting patiently
for you, to feed you. Fledge you, like a plover chick, nesting safely
by shells or driftwood or clumps of seaweed, new to life, insatiably hungry.

An Old Song Replayed

You'll never know how many dreams I've dreamed about you.

Once you've left it, youth's a country you can't renew or return
to. Old friends are living elsewhere, too, or have died while you
were away. Roads, streets you shouldn't need maps to learn
freshly are a maze, your town no longer the place you knew

but a labyrinth with no way out, like woods you'd roamed in freely,
eager to get lost in, that scare you now, pathless and pitch-dark.
Remember how I'd park the car, lights out, by the lake to see
how long it'd take before you'd hold my hand? A horned lark,

a killdeer, a robin might be singing before I'd drive you home.
Or the motel, the smell of mildew on the sheets, in the shower,
five dollars an hour off Route 401, the coffee in the styrofoam
mugs? I should have found a cleaner place to hide in. Or safer.

I traveled further than you ever could, tried to meet you somewhere
alone on my few trips back, both still young, in our mid-twenties.
But you'd married. Fantasies, like the mist breath makes in cold air,
dissipated by news of your wedding, your unwritten letters, my unspoken pleas.

The slow rural road your family's ancient house sat by has become
a busy highway. No loves can compete with the ones age conjures up,
the cows drowsing near us as we took our first daring sips of rum
mixed with RC Cola I'd carefully pour into our shared paper cup.

Your fingers touch my face, trace my lips. Who pays the greater price,
the one who leaves or the one who stays? Wasted days are a crime
against youth, but lost years like to dream. Kiss me once, then kiss me twice,
then kiss me once again. It's been a long, long time.

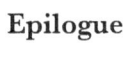

Epilogue

Penelope, Weaving

As she works, her loom sounds like the sea
lapping on beaches, pebbles pinging,
caves in the cliffs echoing breezes'
sighing, her maids gossiping by a door.

The waiting, the painful delay of her life,
daytime weaving, the counterpoint
of thread within thread, by night the music
of its unmaking, softer than sleeping.

The scene she repeats of his returning,
of Argos dying, of her embracing him.
mist enfolding them like a cloud a god
sends to save his favored from death.

Thgkk, thgkk goes the shuttle. She's weaving
out of yearning, out of need, as hungry
as a spider spinning its web, longing
to catch the past, to trap it in her tapestry,

to restore him by what she fabricates
to end her waiting, though he has left
to meet a fate more mortal than Troy's,
wandering where nothing woven in cloth

could ensnare him as she'd hoped before.
Homeless, parched, sun-blistered, roaming
deserts for a place to plant his oar,
he's the madness of passion, the love inside her.

All her suitors are sadly dead. And she,
unraveling at night what she weaves by day,
shuttle renewing the intricate fabric
she afterward ruins, who is she if not made

and unmade by the memories she creates only
to undo them, how they return by leaving,
the weft over and under the warp
threaded, unthreaded, never to be finished.

From Catullus 101

In wayward imagination, I have traveled over
many lands, crossed many oceans
and where has it brought me, brother?
Only to the funeral rites, the devotions
due to those who have died, to their ashes,
oblivious and insensate though they are.
What dark destiny, what fatal star,
led me here against my wishes
and hopes, took you from me, robbed me
of your love? I bring you gifts the past
and our ancestors insist I offer you. Do you see
my tears? Of course you don't, you're dead, I know.
All the more reason, unashamed, I let them flow
so freely. Oh my friend, this bitter grave is the last

place I will ever greet you or meet you again.
Living is the endless revising of a life,
like a poem, in which nearing its completion
you find the unfinishable thing, the line
that is its death. Hail to you and farewell, my brother.

In Place of a Palinode: Improvisations on Four Ancient Poets

1. Xenophanes

If you'll answer my question before it's
too late, I'll ready the setting you've
yearned for. A bowl with cut pink
peonies, yellow roses, a score of lilies.
On a porcelain dish, an apple, a ripe pear.

A fresh breeze blowing through an open
window, a dog frolicking outside, its joy
like yours when you were a boy, playing.
Titmice, a chickadee, finches on the wing,
a wood dove in a tree, mournfully singing.

I'll lay out a white linen tablecloth, on which
I'll rest a bottle the sun shines through,
throwing a swath of prismatic colors
onto a plain white wall. Let us drink wine,
eat cake, dance a while. Death tests us all.

How old were you when the wars began,
ravaging the land, laying waste to
our city? Now you lie under wind-
blown grass, quiet as a stone.
Yet tell me, Pythagoras, why do I still

desire to hold you in my empty arms?
Why do I call you back to bed
every morning as the sun returns
or light a lamp each night while I
glaze your chest and arms with oil?

2. *Alcaeus*

Let us drink and stay drunk forever, Melanippos.
Why aspire to be great? Every line I ever wrote
feels fraudulent, unreal late in my life. I wince
with shame reading them, only myself to blame.

No one masters his fate. Why hope for fame?
When a storm is over, torches glow near ports
and harbors, riotous with workers at the end
of their day's labors, raucous with happiness.

In every broken bit of darkness fallen, death awaits
us, ashen and black, like the beach after great
storms attack the coast and sea and sky
flow into one another; like oblivion descending upon

us. Now, let us cross Acheron, the river no one
travels on twice. Soon, the dog star will wheel
in the sky, auguring summer's parching heat,
the steady beat of cicada's throbbing cries

answering the artichokes' flowering. One last
time, I'm yours, Melanippos. Gaze into
my eyes as we journey together, your ardor,
outpacing Charon's as he works his boat's mighty oars.

3. *An Anonymous Gnostic Poet*

An oak grove, a temple's marble columns casting
long shadows. Like muffled, thrumming drums,
waves roll in. Here, foes are no longer foes,
enemies no longer enemies. Mist-thin clouds,
summer sounds, crickets, cicadas, birds' dawn-
inspired harmonies. A girl dries her hair by its

115

warmth. The ground of being intimated by
the everyday, its care-free beauty. A boy wearing
a plain tunic stares at another with myrtle eyes.
Their consummated music. Translucent as alabaster,
limestone cliffs shimmer while a soft breeze blows
off the sea. A pelican drifts on its slow currents.
More shadows fall from olive trees gleaming
in the heat. The day is a snake sunning its back
in a dream of innocence. A noon moon shines
over a sea still as a lake while time sleeps, hour after
hour, by the rivers that feed it. Say this is a death
no one need weep or mourn for: a language in which
artifice vanishes and the world and the word become
one, like the sun in its first light's splendor, harbinger
of unspoken things never beheld before its gift of a new creation.

4. *Li Shangyin*

Copper-colored untilled fields. Blood
on stones. Mud frozen to a bitter
ice. What a glacial river never
says. What no winter ever confesses.

A man's thoughts are like flowers
that bloom only for one day.
Hills weed-choked, pastures
full of rocks. Emblems, not medals.

A warrior's unsheathed sword hanging
as a warning on a wall off South
Lane by the Ox-Head Road
familiar ghosts journey on nightly.

The pains of boulders, mountains,
pine, fir, rocks, sunset, the sea
are the agonies of an exiled man.
Trees with shadow-flamed, wounded eyes,

birds with thorns for wings in
the brow of the world, the crow-
like spirits of men's bodies dying
during autumn's bone-cold days when

eastern mountains descend into darkness
to drown in the night-black lake
lying far below black-beaked, glutted
hawks in flight. Fly skyward with them.

The thousand years of peace await
you. Already the fifth watch
sounds its dreams of remotest
partings, the cries that summon you

to be freed, to be where there is no
'when' while you and I sit in the west
window talking of night and peace
and rain, unable to sleep, waiting for morning.

Sea and Sky, Night and Silence, Earth and Gods

1.

Icons: ivy, fox, panther, pard; chanting women;
abundant wine; a quake that defies the iron
grip of tyrants. Ecstasy is madness, an omen
of new blood-letting, we're told. Yet every prison
bar is broken when the boy-god with golden
hair dances. I have heard in sea's waves
crashing on the beach auguries of men's passion,
seen in wind-bent trees, tides penetrating caves
past granite cliffs deities of rapture. Flutes, drums,
crotales alert men gathered round a fosse passing
brimming wine bowls about that it's time to succumb
to pleasure. We can smell oregano, sage, dill burning,
you and I, as our bodies are united, joined,
where we lay like two snakes curled and coiled
round each other, like two lives transfigured into one.

And the next morning (this is not a fantasy, exactly,
but a truth that resembles a happy dream), we felt
as if we were waiting dockside for a ship to carry
us not home but to an unknown island where dwelt
and dwell lost gods. To a strange new joy maybe.
A remote place of marble domed mountains, plane trees,
gold sand, grape must scents, grottos, kouroi, a goat
or two nipping on fennel. A place of kindness, ease,
peace, welcoming us with open doors, a sail boat,
swallows flying past our bedroom's sea-salted windows
as noon follows noon and the sun casts no shadows.
Let us stay here. It is a hot night in which we bloom,
flourish best like the phlox and jasmine you planted
in our garden to praise the ancient gods who long ago fled
from Olympus into our fraught seas and skies and passionate bodies.

2.

Under the coruscating glare of reason, all gods flee
into the safety of darkness, dream, nightmare.
Past midnight, a surprising storm from the sea
brings rain battering roofs and windows. I stare
out and see on a neighbor's porch a stone
Buddha burning a candle despite the winds. A steel-
like smell taints the air. Perhaps it's the ozone
from the steady lightning. I want to be in it, to feel
it, the storm and all it is, its power, how it belittles
me, subdues my pride. The crashing waves' mist
mingles with the rain obscuring the beach. The riddles
of life are unsolvable. The madness in the midst
of a tempest, the fit of humanity in it, Lear's rage
against the gods for not existing or being only cruel.
Picking up, the winds put out the candle, erase the sage-
like look on Buddha's face while shadows play me for a fool
as they creep across the ceiling like ghosts or whatever
is left from a storm I'll remember best for my fear when it's over.

3.

The surfers in their wet suits look like puppets
in a shadow play. The sky is flat and gray
like an old ceramic plate. Fishermen cast nets
into the waves, like an image of a misty day
and a tumbling sea in a Hokusai print. The world,
though constantly changing, sometime appears
timeless as art work in a museum. What hurled
us here from nowhere? In this place, where years
pass by us senselessly? Sunlight glitters off a tide-
pool so dark beneath my feet it looks deep. I remember,
five decades ago, swimming in the roiling waters

of the Neuse River in Carolina, alone, no one beside
me to save me as I dived, plunging deeper and deeper
down to touch bottom to uproot a reed to prove I had done
it, but I got nothing, just mud, a slimy rotting weed, no flower
like that Gilgamesh found and lost, his last hope for immortality gone.

4.

Do you recall the chilly night I watched you
standing motionless on a treeless hill
in west Marin, staring toward an invisible
ocean? The moon had set, the stars
were dim, and the sky, like your back,
was black as the unseen sea or the bleak
view one gets of the universe, still and empty
of meaning, in the gaps between stars or galaxies.
You looked like a marble statue or a tall, runic,
indecipherable stone. What was ours in such
blank darkness? In the silhouette of your back
you turned toward me, you seemed to have been
cut from the sky like a swatch or remnant of fabric.
I wanted to join you, knowing you were slowly fading
out of sight into the mystery of night the night we parted.

5.

Coyotes nightly menace the western edge of the park.
The sea beats against its cement barriers.
A child was saved from the Pacific's icy waters
near here yesterday. In the quickening dark,
raccoons squabble on a Chain of Lakes island.
Ravens squawk. Gulls cry. A wailing
drunk rails against the gods, tosses sand

into the air, accosts stragglers at Judah
and La Playa where they are hopelessly waiting
for a handout. This is a metaphysics
of mist and fog. Streetlights glowing a silvery gray
that undoes moonlight. An unseen shopping cart clicks
past on the sidewalk. A crow or someone as hungry
is scrounging invisibly through trash on a night like rain in its clarity.

6.

Laden with massive crates,
two cargo ships rest
by the Golden Gate's
portal. The bay is dark
as pitch or tar. West-
bound, two ships embark
from harbor, hard
to see in the headlands'
shadows despite the mast-
heads and the red sidelights.
Penumbral, metaphysical matters, a shard
inscribed with things and gods long past.
Long ships. Or the triremes Xenophon writes
of. This sea I stand by wanting to understand
these old conundrums. These ancient, hallowed strands.

7.

Half light, half dark, sunset is hesitant.
Three surfers carrying their boards skip
onto the beach, out of the water.
A woman throws driftwood sticks
for her dog to catch. A boat with a searchlight

scans the waves, persistent

in whatever it's looking for. Rip-

tide warnings are posted about the dangers

of the sea tonight. The dog licks

his friend's face. A boy jogs out of sight

into dense fog at the bend of the coastline

where cliffs juts into the ocean at the end of the continent.

This must be what Catullus meant.

Run, run

after him, after life while there's still some sun.

www.ingramcontent.com/pod-product-compliance
Lightning Source LLC
Chambersburg PA
CBHW021207130626
46554CB00005B/2019